Cahoots Too

The Next Cookbook from the Central Coast's Premier Caterers!

by Lisa Jones & Jim Subject

CAHOOTS TOO

CONTENTS

ACKNOWLEDGEMENTS — page 5

INTRODUCTION
by Lisa Jones — page 7

CHAPTER 1
Appetizers & Soups — page 8

CHAPTER 2
Salads — page 36

CHAPTER 3
Vegetables & Sides — page 52

CHAPTER 4
Pasta, Breads & Sandwiches — page 82

CHAPTER 5
Entrées — page 112

CHAPTER 6
Desserts — page 146

CHAPTER 7
Basics — page 168

INDEX — page 178

TABLE OF EQUIVALENTS — page 186

GLOSSARY — page 188

Acknowledgements

I was certain that once I committed to writing the next cookbook that it would be a much easier, more fluid and relaxed project, with the original team in place, a no brainer? But life changes for everyone involved, myself included, and things just can't be taken for granted. That said, we all again stepped up to do our very best and I can't thank our original "A" Team enough for all their efforts.

Before I give my accolades to the team I have to thank the new entry to the acknowledgements and that is all of you who supported the first book *Cahoots Cookbook* published in 2006. It was your constant comments, reviews and appreciation, from coast to coast, and across the globe, (literally, Canada, France, Germany and Poland that I am aware of) for this little self-published cookbook, that makes it truly an honor and frankly a challenge to hopefully meet your expectations for this new book.

Again, thanks to Ron Bez who took the majority of the "Food Glam Photography", or as we fondly call it the "Food Porn", that truly help make this book what it is. Again, thank you Janice Solomon-Webb who worked above and beyond to create and design the layout of this book along with her addition of hand drawn illustrations. And again a special shout out to Katy Budge who is the "Rock" for all her efforts in additional photography, copywriting, editing, and keeping things calm but decisive when things seem impossible. We can't forget our recipe testers, another amazing effort, with a very special thank you to Kasia, who was my other right hand in recipe testing (many of her dishes were photographed), for her patience and support!

Thank you all for an awesome job once again, well done!

Lisa & Jim

Introduction

It seems as if the ink had barely dried on our first publishing effort, *Cahoots Cookbook: Recipes from the Central Coast's Premier Catering Company*, and our customers, much to my surprise, were asking for the next one. After much procrastination, unintentional stalling and unkept promises, we went back to work on *Cahoots Too: The Next Cookbook from the Central Coast's Premier Caterers!*.

Over the years we have certainly tried to keep up with the latest tastes and trends, but I can't remember a time when there's been such a juxtaposition of them on the table at once – from certified organic to GMOs, from farm-to-table to molecular gastronomy, from locovores to celebrity chefs, from everything sustainable to everything microwaveable. It's fun and challenging, but likely a sign of the times.

In this book, I believe we have achieved a nice balance of our tried-and-true local favorites along with some fun, delicious and interesting ingredients from all over the world. With the explosion of available ingredients through the internet and specialty stores we are now – more than ever – able to treat ourselves to new flavor profiles. We have also included several recipes that are gluten free, vegetarian and vegan, as these are requests we deal with on a daily basis.

Jim and I both believe that the best results are achieved when you start with quality products, fresh ingredients, dedication, consistency and supporting your local community. It's not rocket science, but more of a mantra that has served us (and our clients) very well over the past 23 years in business. We value all the appreciation and support we've gotten from our customers and friends over the years, and hope to give a little bit back in *Cahoots Too*. And yes, we are finally giving you the recipes for such longtime favorites as the Thai Salad Dressing and the Chipotle Mayonnaise, "so enjoy"!

Chapter 1
APPETIZERS & SOUPS

Crispy Prosciutto Crostini
with Caramelized Onion & Pecorino
    page **18**

Mediterranean Quesadilla page **20**

Asian Chicken Bundles
with Thai Dipping Sauce page **22**

Grilled Chicken Spiedini page **24**

Golden Gazpacho page **26**

Winter Squash Soup
with Cheesy Crouton page **28**

Sesame Chicken Skewers
with Roasted Garlic
Lemon Aioli page **10**

Beef Empanadas
with Aji Panca Sauce page **12**

Herb Salad Spring Rolls
with Dipping Sauce page **14**

Artichoke Leek Squares page **16**

Shiitake Mushroom
Spring Rolls page **17**

Asparagus Soup
with Goat Cheese & Lemon
Crème Fraîche page **30**

Pumpkin Bisque
with White Cheddar
Sage Cheese page **31**

French Onion Soup
with Grilled Gruyere
Sandwiches page **32**

Cahoots Corn Chowder page **34**

Brandied Roasted Chestnut Soup
with Fennel Confit page **35**

Cahoots Too

Sesame Chicken Skewers
with Roasted Garlic Lemon Aioli

This appetizer has been a staple on our catering menu for years.

1½ pounds chicken tenders or chicken breasts cut into 3" long, ½" wide pieces

½ cup white wine

½ cup light soy sauce

½ cup sesame oil

2 tablespoons seasoned rice wine vinegar

4 cloves garlic, chopped

2 teaspoons salt

1 teaspoon fresh ground pepper

2 cups raw sesame seeds

Lemon Aioli, page 174

½ cup roasted garlic, reserve 1 tablespoon for garnish

30 8" wooden skewers

1. Carefully weave one piece of chicken onto each wooden skewer. Arrange in a 13" x 9" x 2" baking dish.

2. In a bowl, mix together white wine, soy sauce, sesame oil, rice wine vinegar, garlic, salt and pepper and stir well. Pour over the chicken skewers and marinate for 8 hours or overnight.

Preheat oven to 350° F.

3. Lay the chicken skewers onto a baking sheet. Generously sprinkle with sesame seeds then flip them to coat the other side.

4. Make one recipe Lemon Aioli (page 174), add the roasted garlic. Pulse to blend.

5. Bake the chicken skewers for 10-12 minutes until fully cooked and lightly browned. Serve with Roasted Garlic Lemon Aioli.

Makes 30 skewers or enough for 18-20

CHAPTER 1 • APPETIZERS & SOUPS

Serve with a crisp white Rhône

Beef Empanadas
with Aji Panca Sauce

I have been on a Pan American cooking craze, especially Peruvian. I was in a Peruvian restaurant in Southern California and fell in love with the Aji Panca Sauce. I tried everything possible to get any part of the recipe but failed miserably. The one thing I did know was they used Aji Amarillo, a yellow chile used extensively throughout Peru. This is my attempt at the recipe, it is a lot of work with hard to find ingredients, but, if you are as OCD as me when it comes to great salsas and sauces this should be worth the effort.

EMPANADA DOUGH

2 cups all-purpose flour

¼ cup unsalted butter, cubed and very cold or frozen

1 teaspoon baking powder

1 teaspoon salt

⅓ cup water

1 tablespoon white vinegar

Empanada Filling
recipe next page

Oil for frying

Aji Panca, page 171

TO MAKE THE DOUGH

1. Add the flour, salt, baking powder, and butter to the food processor fitted with a steel blade. Add the vinegar to the water and with the machine running slowly add the liquid until the dough forms a ball. Remove from the work bowl, cover and let rest 30 minutes.

Chapter 1 • Appetizers & Soups

EMPANADA FILLING
2 cups shredded beef
I like to use leftover short rib meat (the best) or I also like to cut up cooked Tri-Tip or other flavorful cut of meat in the crock pot with a little beef stock and house seasoning on low for about 8 hours. This meat is also great in enchiladas and taquitos.

1 cup jalapeño Jack, Munster or Chihuahua cheese, shredded

¼ cup green onions, chopped

½ teaspoon dried oregano

½ teaspoon cumin

½ teaspoon sweet paprika

Salt & pepper to taste

Egg wash (1 egg and ¼ cup water)

To make the Filling

1. Combine shredded beef, cheese, onions and spices, mix well, set aside.

To assemble the Empanadas

1. Roll dough out on a floured surface. Using a 3" round cutter, cut the dough into 24 rounds and cover with plastic. On a floured surface roll each ball into a thin round. Add a heaping teaspoon of filling to the center, moisten one edge of the circle, fold in half and crimp with a fork, careful not to break the seal. Can be made ahead, covered and refrigerated or frozen, bring to room temperature before frying.

2. In a frying pan heat ½ inch of oil to 350° F. Add a few empanadas at a time, don't crowd them, and cook for a couple of minutes on both sides until golden brown. Drain on paper towels and serve immediately with aji panca or other favorite dipping sauce or salsa.

Makes 24 small Empanadas

Serve with a Tempranillo

CAHOOTS TOO

Herb Salad Spring Rolls
with Dipping Sauce

I taught cooking classes at a little gourmet kitchen shop we had in Paso Robles years ago called The Cook's Loft. These are from a class about all things wrapped. I personally love these, especially on a hot summer day; they are light, refreshing and good for you. Don't be afraid to be generous with the herbs, the combination is great.

2 ounces bean-thread noodles

2 tablespoons seasoned rice wine vinegar

1 tablespoon sriracha or Asian chili sauce

16 8" rice paper rounds

16 Boston lettuce leaves

1 bunch green onions, washed, trimmed and chopped

1 cup carrot, grated

1 cup Napa cabbage, finely shredded

½ cup red bell pepper, diced

1 ounce each, fresh basil, mint and cilantro leaves

½ cup chopped toasted nuts (cashews, peanuts, almonds or any combination)

1. In a bowl soak noodles in very hot water for 5-6 minutes. Drain well and chop into 3-4 inch pieces. Toss in vinegar and sriracha and set aside.

2. Pour warm water into a 9" cake pan or similar sized pan slightly larger than rice paper. Add the rice paper, one at a time to the water and let soak for about 15 seconds or until pliable. When the first rice paper wrapper is ready, transfer to a work surface. In the center of the paper, divide the noodles, lettuce leaves, green onions, carrots, Napa cabbage, pepper, herb leaves and nuts, evenly among the wrappers. Fold the sides in, then roll the wrapper up, like a burrito, so the filling can't fall out. Repeat with remaining wrappers. Serve with your favorite dipping sauce, I like the Thai dressing on page 50.

Serves 6-8

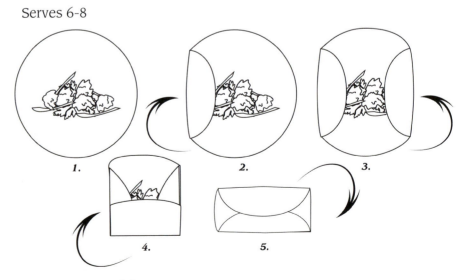

CHAPTER 1 • APPETIZERS & SOUPS

Cahoots Too

Artichoke Leek Squares

This is one of those old school, need something quick, kind of recipe. It is easy and can be done ahead with a quick 10 minute warm up before serving.

- 2   6-ounce jars of marinated artichoke hearts
- 1½ cups leeks, thinly sliced and washed
- 2 cloves garlic, chopped
- 5 eggs
- ⅓ cup good quality bread crumbs
- ¼ cup fresh parsley, chopped
- ½ teaspoon Italian seasoning
- ½ teaspoon red pepper flakes (optional)
- ¼ pound Munster cheese, grated
- ¼ pound sharp cheddar cheese, grated
- 3 tablespoons Parmesan cheese, grated

Preheat oven to 325° F, grease an 8" x 8" baking dish

1. Drain the artichoke hearts marinade into a sauté pan. Heat the marinade over medium heat. Add the leeks and garlic and cook until soft, about 5 minutes. Remove from heat and let cool.

2. In a bowl beat the eggs. Coarsely chop the artichoke hearts and add to the egg mixture. Stir in remaining ingredients and mix well. Spread onto a greased baking sheet and bake for 25- 30 minutes.

3. Let rest until cool enough to cut into squares and serve.

Serves 12-14

Chapter 1 • Appetizers & Soups

Shiitake Mushroom Spring Rolls

2 tablespoons olive/canola oil blend

8 cloves garlic, chopped

2 cups leeks, sliced and washed

1 tablespoon fresh ginger root, peeled and minced

2-3 serrano chiles, minced

4 cups shiitake mushrooms or combination of shiitake, button, cremini, etc., sliced

½ cup hoisin sauce

1 3-ounce package of bean thread noodles

1 cup bean sprouts

1 cup green onions, chopped

½ cup cilantro, chopped

1 package of egg roll wrappers

Egg wash, (1 egg and ¼ cup water whisked together)

Oil for frying

1. Heat oil in a sauté pan over medium high heat, add garlic, leeks, ginger root, chiles, stir quickly for about 1 minute. Add the mushrooms, stir quickly being careful not to burn, about a minute. Add the hoisin sauce and bean sprouts, lower heat to medium and simmer about 1 minute stirring often. Drain and cool in strainer.

2. Prepare bean thread noodles by soaking in a bowl of very hot water for 15 minutes. Drain well and chop into 3-4" pieces.

3. When the filling has cooled, transfer to a bowl and add the green onions, cilantro and bean threads. Mix well.

4. Lay out one egg roll wrapper and place a heaping tablespoon of filling at the bottom of the wrapper closet to you. Moisten edges with egg wash and roll bottom towards the middle, fold on both sides and continue rolling. *See diagram on page 14.* Repeat with remaining wrappers.

5. Deep fry at 350° F until golden brown, drain on paper towels. Serve with your favorite dipping sauce.

Serves 8-10, makes about 26-28 rolls

Cahoots Too

Crispy Prosciutto Crostini
with Caramelized Onion & Pecorino

This recipe can be adapted many ways, a lot like pizza or flat bread. I like to do a variety of different crostinis to mix it up a little.

½ pound prosciutto, thinly sliced then cut into strips

2 tablespoons butter

2 tablespoons good quality olive oil

1½ pounds sweet onions, thinly sliced

2 tablespoons fresh thyme leave, chopped

2 cups Pecorino cheese, grated

1 sourdough baguette, sliced to 24 ½" pieces

Olive oil for brushing

Preheat oven to 350° F.

1. Add prosciutto to a frying pan with a little bit of olive oil. Fry, stirring often, until crisp and lightly browned. Drain on paper towels.

2. Melt the butter and olive oil together. Add the onions and cook over medium low heat, stirring occasionally, until they are golden brown. Stir in thyme leaves. Cool mixture.

3. Mix together the onions, cheese and prosciutto.

4. Place the sliced baguettes onto a baking sheet. Brush lightly with olive oil. Divide the onion mixture onto the baguette slices and bake for 6-8 minutes or until golden brown and bubbly.

Serves 6-8

Chapter 1 • Appetizers & Soups

Serve with a Sangiovese

Cahoots Too

Mediterranean Quesadilla

If you can find spinach and tomato flavored tortillas along with regular flour tortillas, it is fun to mix up the colors. There are lots of options to play with here so feel free to improvise.

3 12" flour tortillas

1 tablespoon olive oil

1 cup Tapenade, page 173

4-5 cups shredded mozzarella cheese

1 cup sun dried tomatoes in oil, drained and coarsely chopped

¼ pound thinly sliced salami (I like Finocchiona, Tuscan orange-wild fennel salami)

5 ounces baby arugula

¾ cup feta cheese, crumbled

½ cup Basil Pesto, page 175

Sour cream

1. In a 14" frying pan over medium heat add 1 teaspoon of olive oil. Spread ¼ cup olive tapenade onto each tortilla. One at a time add the tortillas to the pan, tapenade side up. Sprinkle the entire tortilla with 1½ cups of shredded mozzarella. On one half of the tortilla add ⅓ cup sun dried tomatoes and a third of the salami. To the other half of the tortilla add ¼ cup feta cheese and a third of the arugula.

2. With a spatula, carefully fold the tortilla in half at the division of ingredients. Lower heat and cook for about 2 minutes. Flip and cook an additional 2 minutes watching them carefully so they don't burn.

3. Remove from pan with spatula or gently slide them onto a cutting board. Repeat with the next two tortillas.

4. Slice each quesadilla into six wedges, serve with basil pesto and sour cream, or mix the pesto with the sour cream.

Serves 8-10

CHAPTER 1 • APPETIZERS & SOUPS

Serve with a Merlot

Cahoots Too

Asian Chicken Bundles
with Thai Dipping Sauce

This is another great use for the Thai Salad Dressing on page 50 and another great use of rice paper that you may have invested in for the herb spring rolls on page 14.

- 1 pound ground chicken
- 2 teaspoons salt
- 2 teaspoons fresh ground pepper
- ¼ cup garlic chili paste
- ⅓ cup sesame seeds
- ¼ cup hoisin sauce
- 4 cloves garlic, chopped
- 16 green onions, trimmed and chopped
- 24 rice paper rounds
- 24 sprigs cilantro
- Vegetable oil for frying
- Thai Salad Dressing, page 50

1. In a bowl combine the ground chicken, spices, garlic chili paste, sesame seeds, hoisin sauce, garlic and green onions, mix well. Prepare the rice paper as instructed on page 14, step 2.

2. To assemble lay out softened rice paper. Add a sprig of cilantro to the center. Top with ¼ cup chicken mixture. Fold the bottom edge of the rice paper over the chicken, then fold down the top edge. Flip, then flatten the bundle and tuck the sides underneath, so it will cook evenly, enclose completely. Repeat with remaining rice papers.

3. In a frying pan add ½" of vegetable oil and heat to 350° F. Add the bundles and cook in batches, seam side first, about 3 minutes a side until golden brown and cooked through. Drain on paper towels. Keep warm until ready to serve. Serve with Thai Salad Dressing as dipping sauce.

Serves 8-10

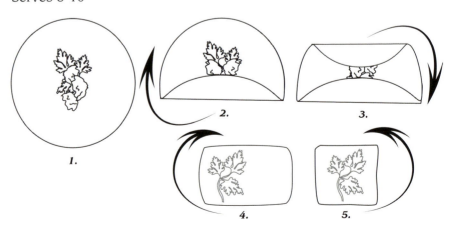

Chapter 1 • Appetizers & Soups

Serve with a crisp white Rhône or dry Gewürztraminer

Cahoots Too

Grilled Chicken Spiedini

Spiedini is an Italian word for "skewers of meat". Its origin is Sicilian, influenced by the medieval Arab era. I have seen so many variations, but this is one we have done for years at the annual Tobin James Cellars Mediterranean Festival. We make nearly a thousand of them and always run out. If you are feeling super ambitious, make the caramelized onion focaccia on page 88 to put on the skewers. Enjoy!

1 pound ground chicken

1 egg

½ cup pecorino cheese, grated

2 cloves garlic, minced

½ cup fresh ground sourdough bread crumbs

2 tablespoons fresh parsley, chopped

½ teaspoon salt

½ teaspoon fresh ground pepper

½ teaspoon dried oregano

½ loaf good quality Italian bread like focaccia or ciabatta, cut into 10 1" cubes

Good quality olive oil for grilling and drizzling

10 7" wooden skewers, soaked in water

1. In a mixing bowl, combine ground chicken, egg, pecorino, garlic, bread crumbs, parsley, and seasonings. Mix well.

2. Make 20 meatballs from the chicken mixture, they don't need to be perfect, just uniform in size, as you will be molding them onto the skewer.

3. Take a skewer and add a meatball, than a piece of bread and then another meatball. You will finish the shaping on the skewer. Repeat with remaining skewers.

4. Prepare a charcoal, wood or gas grill to medium heat. Lightly brush the spiedini with olive oil.

5. Place the skewers on the grill, watch for flare ups if your fire is too hot, and grill turning 2-3 times or as needed, until meat is cooked through and bread is golden, about 15 minutes. Drizzle with olive oil and serve.

Serves 6-8

Chapter 1 • Appetizers & Soups

Cahoots Too

Golden Gazpacho

This recipe works well in the summer when you have access to vine ripe yellow tomatoes. If you have the first Cahoots Cookbook there is a recipe for White Gazpacho. On special occasions I like to serve a trio of gazpachos...White, Golden and Red (or traditional gazpacho). I like to serve them in shot glasses for a beautiful presentation and variation.

2 cloves garlic

½ cucumber, peeled and chopped

1 cup sour cream

4 yellow tomatoes, diced

1 cup fresh or frozen corn kernels (thawed)

½ sweet yellow onion, finely diced

1 yellow bell pepper, seeded and finely diced

¼ cup vegetable stock

1 tablespoon parsley, chopped

4 tablespoons extra virgin olive oil, preferably lemon flavored

1 teaspoon salt

½ teaspoon pepper

1 cup pumpkin seeds or pepitas

1 tablespoon olive oil (lemon flavored is good here too)

1 teaspoon salt

1. Chop the garlic in the food processor. Add the cucumber and puree for about 30 seconds. Add the sour cream and puree mixture until smooth. Transfer to a mixing bowl.

2. Add the tomatoes, corn, onion, yellow bell peppers, stock, parsley, olive oil, salt and pepper. Mix well.

3. Heat 1 tablespoon of olive oil in a sauté pan. Add pumpkin seeds and stir continuously until they start to pop and brown. Pull them from the heat and cool, toss with salt.

4. Garnish gazpacho with toasted pumpkin seeds.

Serves 6-8 or fills 25-30 shot glasses

Chapter 1 • Appetizers & Soups

CAHOOTS TOO

Winter Squash Soup
with Cheesy Crouton

Every fall we do a wine club event at J. Lohr Vineyards that involves a Fall inspired soup and every year I have to come up with a soup to rival the previous year's soup. Not an easy task, with high expectations; this was last year's recipe.

SOUP
½ stick of butter

5 cloves garlic

1 large sweet yellow onion

6 quarts vegetable stock

4 pounds or about 10 cups assorted winter squash, preferably butternut, acorn, or kombucha, peeled and diced in 1" pieces

1 teaspoon Herbs de Provence

5 fresh sage leaves or 1 teaspoon dried

2 teaspoons ground turmeric

½ teaspoon ground ginger

1 tablespoon salt

2 teaspoons poultry seasoning

1 teaspoon nutmeg

¼ whipping cream

FOR THE SOUP
Preheat oven to 350° F.

1. Melt the butter in a stock pot over medium heat. Add garlic and onion and sauté for about 8 minutes or until tender. Add vegetable stock, winter squash and herbs and spices. Cover and simmer until squash is very tender, about 30 minutes.

2. Working in small batches carefully puree the soup in blender or food processor. Return to stock pot. Stir in cream, season with salt and pepper and bring to a simmer. Can be made a day ahead, chilled and reheated over medium heat.

Chapter 1 • Appetizers & Soups

CROUTONS
2 tablespoons olive oil

1 sourdough baguette, sliced into 24 ¼" slices

1 cup Gruyere cheese, grated

2 teaspoons Herbs de Provence

FOR THE CROUTONS
1. Brush the bread slices with olive oil, top with Herbs de Provence, salt and pepper. Bake for about 10 minutes. Sprinkle with cheese and bake until cheese melts, about 5 minutes. Serve soup topped with cheesy croutons.

Serves 8-10

Cahoots Too

Asparagus Soup
with Goat Cheese & Lemon Crème Fraîche

2 tablespoons olive oil

1 cup sweet onion, chopped

2 cloves garlic, chopped

1 stalk celery, chopped

2 Yukon gold potatoes, diced

6 cups vegetable stock

2 pounds asparagus, cut into 1" pieces, discard tough ends

Salt and pepper to taste

½ cup cream

½ cup crème fraîche

½ cup goat cheese crumbles

1 lemon, zested and juiced

Fresh chives for garnish

1. In a stock pot, heat oil over medium heat. Add onion, garlic, celery and potatoes. Sauté the vegetables until they start to soften, about 5 minutes, stirring often. Add the stock and bring soup up to a simmer. Add the asparagus, continue cooking until the asparagus is starting to get tender, about 3-4 minutes.

2. Using an immersion blender (or standard blender – carefully working in batches), puree soup. Add the cream and season to taste with salt and pepper.

3. Stir together the crème fraîche, goat cheese crumbles, lemon zest and juice and set aside. Serve garnished with a spoonful of the goat cheese & lemon crème fraîche and fresh chives.

Serves 6-8

CHAPTER 1 • APPETIZERS & SOUPS

Pumpkin Bisque
with White Cheddar Sage Cheese

I use a white cheddar sage cheese from Bravo Farms in California (www.bravofarms.com). If you can't get that try substituting white cheddar cheese and ground sage.

- 5 ounces bacon, chopped
- 2 ounces shallots, chopped
- 2 cups pumpkin puree
- 3 cups chicken stock
- 3 fresh sage leaves, chopped
- ½ teaspoon black pepper
- ½ teaspoon ginger
- ¼ teaspoon nutmeg
- ½ teaspoon salt
- ½ teaspoon crushed red pepper
- 1 tablespoon lemon juice
- ¼ cup whipping cream
- 1-2 cups white cheddar sage cheese, shredded

1. Add bacon to a stock pot over medium heat. Cook bacon until it starts to crisp and most of the fat has rendered out.

2. Add the shallots and sauté for a couple of minutes. Add the rest of the ingredients except the cream and cheese, and simmer for about 20 minutes over low heat.

3. Remove the pot from the heat and carefully puree the mixture with a immersion blender (or standard blender-carefully working in batches) until smooth. Return to heat and stir in cream. Serve with a sprinkling of white cheddar sage cheese.

Serves 6-8

Cahoots Too

French Onion Soup
with Grilled Gruyere Sandwiches

The secret to great French onion soup is cooking the onions low and slow until they are a deep, dark golden color, and the sandwich is just icing on the cake. The problem I have with this soup is waiting for it to get cool enough to eat.

SOUP
- 2 tablespoons good quality olive oil
- ½ cup unsalted butter
- 8 cups sweet yellow onions, thinly sliced (about 4 large)
- 2 shallots, chopped
- 4 cloves garlic, chopped
- 2 tablespoon fresh thyme leaves
- 4 tablespoons flour
- 2 tablespoon Dijon mustard
- ½ cup brandy or cognac
- 6 cups beef stock
- ½ teaspoon fresh ground black pepper
- ¼ teaspoon ground nutmeg

SANDWICHES
- 1 sourdough or French baguette
- ½ pound good quality Swiss cheese such as Gruyere, sliced
- 2 tablespoons butter for grilling sandwiches

FOR THE SOUP

1. Heat oil and butter until bubbly, add the onions. Cook over medium low heat, covered, stirring often, about 20 minutes. Add the garlic, shallot and thyme, cook for an additional 10 minutes until deep golden brown. Add the flour and cook stirring often for 3 minutes. Add the mustard, brandy, beef stock, pepper and nutmeg. Cover and simmer for about 15-20 minutes.

FOR THE SANDWICHES

2. While the soup is finishing slice the baguette on the bias into 24 slices and lay them out. Generously top 12 of the bread slices with cheese, top with other piece of bread and pat firmly.

3. Melt the butter in a large skillet until bubbly. Add the sandwiches and grill until they are golden brown and crispy on each side, flipping once.

Serves 6-8

Chapter 1 • Appetizers & Soups

Serve with a Cabernet Sauvignon or Bordeaux blend (typically Cabernet Sauvignon/ Cabernet Franc/Merlot)

Cahoots Too

Cahoots Corn Chowder

This was a favorite in our restaurant years ago. You can add diced cooked chicken and crispy tortilla strips at the end and transform this soup into Chicken Tortilla Soup.

- ¼ pound bacon, chopped
- 2 cups sweet white onion, diced
- 1 pound Yukon Gold potatoes, washed and diced
- 1 cup celery, chopped (about 3 stalks)
- 2 Poblano peppers, seeded, deveined and diced
- 1 carrot, peeled and diced
- 1 red bell pepper, diced
- 4 cups corn fresh or frozen (fresh is best, you will need about 6-7 ears)
- 4 cups chicken stock, preferably low sodium
- 1 teaspoon salt
- 1 teaspoon fresh ground black pepper
- 1 teaspoon ground cumin
- 1 teaspoon dried oregano
- 5 dashes Tabasco®
- 1 cup heavy cream
- ½ cup fresh cilantro, chopped

1. In a stock pot, cook bacon over medium low heat until starting to crisp. Stir in onions and potatoes, let simmer about a minute. Add celery, peppers, carrots and corn, stir well. Add stock and seasonings, simmer covered for about 20 minutes or until the potatoes are soft.

2. Add the cream, cook an additional 10 minutes. Stir in cilantro and serve.

Serves 6-8

CHAPTER 1 • APPETIZERS & SOUPS

Brandied Roasted Chestnut Soup
with Fennel Confit

This is a lovely holiday soup. I have served this on many occasions at holiday parties as an appetizer in demitasse cups. Also another J. Lohr hit.

SOUP
- 2 cups roasted, shelled and skinned chestnuts or 1 14 ounce bottle
- 4 tablespoons unsalted butter
- 2 shallots, chopped
- 2 leeks, washed and chopped
- ½ fennel bulb, stalks and core removed, chopped
- 2 tablespoons brandy, divided
- 3½ cups vegetable broth
- ¼ cup half and half
- 1 teaspoon fennel pollen* optional

CONFIT
- ½ fennel bulb, stalks and core removed, chopped
- 1 clove garlic, minced
- 1 sprig fresh thyme
- ½ teaspoon salt
- ¼ cup good quality olive oil

FOR THE SOUP
1. Coarsely chop chestnuts in the food processor, set aside.
2. In a stock pot melt butter. Add the shallots and leeks and cook until softened. Add the fennel and stir a minute more. Add the brandy cook a minute more. Add the broth and chestnuts and simmer for about 20 minutes, covered. With a hand held blender or regular blender (in batches) carefully puree soup. Add back to the pot add half and half, fennel pollen and adjust seasoning. Thin with water if needed.

FOR THE CONFIT
1. Thinly slice the fennel. In a small sauce pan add fennel, garlic, thyme, salt and olive oil. Cook over low heat, covered, for about 30 minutes, until soft and luscious.
2. Drain the fennel confit, reserve oil for another use (such as the Layered Two Potato & Fennel Gratin on page 78). Serve soup garnished with fennel confit.

Serves 6-8

*www.pollenranch.com

Chapter 2
SALADS

Lisa's Favorite Salad	page **38**
Cahoots Spinach Salad	page **40**
Good Old Macaroni Salad	page **42**
Heirloom Tomato Salad with Gorgonzola & Kalamata	page **43**
Ensalada Verano (Summer Salad)	page **44**
White Bean, Tomato & Basil Salad	page **46**
Jim's Favorite Salad	page **47**
Grilled Panzanella Salad	page **48**
Fiesta Slaw	page **49**
Cahoots World Famous Thai Chicken Salad	page **50**

CAHOOTS TOO

Lisa's Favorite Salad

We served this salad at a fundraiser for the victims of the Hurricane Katrina in 2008; we served it with grilled chicken breast and it was a huge hit. The dressing is a Tomato, Jalapeño, Mint Vinaigrette that I came up with after enjoying a similar type salad in Los Angeles; this is my version.

TOMATO, JALAPEÑO, MINT VINAIGRETTE DRESSING
- 1 ounce shallot or 1 medium shallot
- 1 ounce fresh jalapeño, seeded and deveined
- ½ ounce or 1 cup fresh mint
- 2 tablespoons tomato paste
- 2 teaspoons Gulden's® Spicy mustard
- ⅓ cup red wine vinegar
- 2 tablespoons seasoned rice wine vinegar
- ½ teaspoon salt
- 1¼ cups olive oil/canola blend

SALAD
- 12 ounces sweet mixed greens, preferably no radicchio or frisee
- ¾ cup Maytag blue cheese or Roquefort-style blue cheese, crumbled
- ¾ cup toasted pepitas (shelled pumpkin seeds)
- 1 cups tortilla strips, fried until crisp and lightly salted
- 1½ cups chopped, cooked chicken breast (optional)

FOR THE DRESSING
1. Add the shallot to a food processor and chop. Add the jalapeño, mint, tomato paste, mustard, red wine vinegar, rice wine vinegar and salt. Blend ingredients for about 15 seconds and then slowly add the olive oil in a steady stream, scrape down sides of bowl and blend until smooth.

FOR THE SALAD
1. Add sweet greens to a salad bowl and toss with about ½ cup dressing, a little more if you are adding chicken. Add the blue cheese, pepitas, tortilla strips and chicken, toss and serve.

Serves 6-8

CHAPTER 2 • SALADS

Cahoots Too

Cahoots Spinach Salad

I love the right combination of sweet, tangy, salty and texture when making spinach salad. It took me a while to get this right but I think I nailed this recipe. Try this salad with chopped grilled chicken for a more substantial entrée salad.

DRESSING

½ ounce shallot or ½ a shallot

1½ teaspoons Dijon mustard

½ cup Cabernet Sauvignon vinegar or other red wine vinegar

2 tablespoons agave syrup

½ teaspoon salt

¼ teaspoon black pepper

¾ cup + 2 tablespoons olive oil/canola blend

SALAD

6 ounces pancetta

1 pound fresh baby spinach

¾ cup goat cheese crumbles

¾ cup pistachios, toasted and coarsely chopped

¾ cup dried cherries

FOR THE DRESSING
1. Add shallot to a food processor and chop. Add the Dijon, vinegar, agave syrup, salt and pepper. Blend for about 15 seconds and slowly add the olive oil until blended.

FOR THE SALAD
1. Chop raw pancetta add to a sauté pan with a splash of olive oil and cook over medium heat until crispy, drain and set aside.

2. Add the spinach to a large salad bowl and toss with dressing, add the cooked pancetta, goat cheese, pistachios, and dried cherries and toss again.

Serves 6-8

Chapter 2 • Salads

Cahoots Too

Good Old Macaroni Salad

I know what you're thinking...macaroni salad? I reluctantly left it out of the first cookbook because, quite frankly, it didn't seem interesting enough. That said, I have to say this is an all-time favorite for not only Jim and me but also many of our loyal customers. It has its place on the table, and reminds me of my father "Radar"; he loved to make it for special occasions and it was a family favorite; he liked to add bay shrimp to his. This is my rendition.

- 1 pound small elbow macaroni
- ½ red onion chopped
- ¼ cup of red wine vinegar
- ½ pound celery, chopped
- 7 hard boiled eggs, sliced
- 1 dill pickle, diced
- 1 cup black olives, sliced
- 2 cups mayonnaise
- 1 tablespoon Dijon mustard
- 1 teaspoon salt
- 1 teaspoon fresh ground black pepper
- 1-2 splashes of Tabasco® sauce

1. Bring water to a boil add macaroni and cook per package instructions. Drain and add to mixing bowl.

2. Marinate the red onion in red wine vinegar for about 10 minutes, and drain. Add to macaroni.

3. Add the rest of the ingredients, mix well and serve immediately or chill 2 hours.

Serves 8-10

CHAPTER 2 • SALADS

Heirloom Tomato Salad
with Gorgonzola & Kalamata

This salad is all about great ingredients. We do this every year at the Tobin James End of Summer Barbeque, when of course tomatoes are bountiful and delicious. Feel free to add your spin to it.

- 10 tomatoes, cored, sliced, preferably colorful and vine-ripened heirloom varieties
- ½ pint micro arugula or fresh baby arugula
- ½ cup Gorgonzola cheese, crumbled
- ½ cup Kalamata olives, pitted and halved
- 2 tablespoons capers
- ½ cup good quality olive oil
- ¼ white balsamic vinegar
- Salt and pepper

1. Arrange the tomatoes on a platter, I like to alternate colors and space them about ½" apart. Top with arugula, Gorgonzola, Kalamata olives and capers. Drizzle with olive oil, balsamic vinegar then sprinkle with salt and pepper. Serve with warm crusty bread.

Serves 8-10

Cahoots Too

Ensalada Verano
(Summer Salad)

My mother makes a summer salad, with the usual suspects... tomato, cucumber, bell pepper, red onion, in vinaigrette. I upped the ante on this and added a Mexican twist. Don't be afraid, this is tried-and-true, on many large occasions. Please feel free to improvise on this recipe, as almost anything summer-ish will work.

SALAD

3 tomatoes, cored and sliced into wedges

1 cucumber, peeled and sliced

1 red onion, peeled and thinly sliced

1 small or ½ large jicama, peeled and julienned

1 red bell pepper, julienned

1 yellow bell pepper, julienned

1 fresh poblano chile (often called Pasilla in the store), julienned

1 fresh New Mexico chile, or Anaheim, julienned

1 jalapeño, seeded and deveined, julienned

½ cup queso fresco or feta cheese, chopped for garnish

DRESSING

3 cloves garlic

1 tablespoon cumin seed, toasted and cooled, then crushed with the back of a knife

½ teaspoon red chili flakes

2 tablespoons cilantro leaves, chopped

3 tablespoons fresh lime juice

1 teaspoon salt

½ cup red wine vinegar

1¼ cups light olive oil or olive oil canola blend

FOR THE DRESSING
1. Add garlic to a food processor. Chop garlic. Add the spices cilantro, salt and red wine vinegar. With the motor running add the oil.

FOR THE SALAD
1. Add all the cut vegetables to a mixing bowl. Toss with dressing. Garnish the top with chopped cheese.

Serves 6-8

CHAPTER 2 • SALADS

Cahoots Too

White Bean, Tomato & Basil Salad

This is so simple and so delicious. We like to serve it with our lasagna or other pasta dishes in addition to a green salad to balance out the meal. It is also a great alternative for a bean dish on a hot summer night. Take advantage of the great heirloom cherry tomatoes that really beautify this dish.

SALAD
3 15½-ounce cans small white beans

2 15½-ounce cans Cannellini beans

2 pints cherry tomatoes (heirlooms or mixed cherry tomatoes if available)

DRESSING
4 cloves garlic

1 teaspoon Dijon mustard

½ tablespoons salt

1 teaspoon black pepper

⅓ cup white balsamic vinegar

¾ cup olive oil/canola blend

1 ounce fresh basil (roughly chopped/ chiffonade)

For the Salad
1. Drain and rinse beans. Put white beans and Cannellini beans in a large bowl and add the cherry tomatoes.

For the Dressing
2. Chop garlic in food processor. Add mustard, salt, pepper, and vinegar. With the machine running slowly add olive oil and blend for about 30 seconds. Add chopped basil and blend for an additional 30 seconds. Pour over white beans and tomatoes and mix.

Serves 10-12

Jim's Favorite Salad

Okay...the truth, I already had a favorite salad, so I named this one after Jim. Don't get me wrong, he really likes it, but it now out sells my favorite salad. Way to go Jim!

SALAD
12 ounces spring mix

¾ cup Rogue Creamery smoked blue cheese or other favorite blue cheese

¾ cup toasted pecans, coarsely chopped

¾ cup dried blueberries

CHIPOTLE VINAIGRETTE
2 cloves garlic

1 small chipotle pepper in adobo + 1 teaspoon of adobo sauce

2 teaspoons Gulden's® Spicy Mustard

2 tablespoons fresh squeezed lime juice

2 tablespoons white balsamic vinegar

¼ cup seasoned rice wine vinegar

½ teaspoon salt

½ teaspoon fresh ground coriander

1¼ cups light olive oil or olive oil/canola blend

FOR THE VINAIGRETTE
1. Add garlic to a food processor and chop.
   Add the chipotle pepper, adobo sauce, mustard, lime juice, white balsamic, rice wine vinegar, salt and coriander. With the machine running, slowly add the oil in a steady stream. Scrape down the sides of the bowl and process until well blended, about a minute.

FOR THE SALAD
1. Add spring mix to a salad bowl. Toss with about ½ cup of the vinaigrette, more or less depending on your taste. Add the rest of the ingredients and serve.

Serves 6-8

CAHOOTS TOO

Grilled Panzanella Salad

Panzanella is a traditional Italian bread salad, invented it to use up leftover or stale bread. Our twist is to grill the bread for the salad, and if available, use a variety of heirloom tomatoes. This is simple to make and is a hearty side.

SALAD

1 loaf ciabatta or focaccia bread, about 1 pound

Olive oil for brushing

Salt and pepper

6 tomatoes, cored and cut into wedges, preferably colorful heirlooms such as Green Zebra, Yellow, and Brandywine to name a few.

1 bunch green onions, chopped

½ cup fresh basil, chiffonade

4-6 garlic cloves, sliced in ½

DRESSING

2 cloves garlic, chopped

¼ cup red wine vinegar

½ cup good quality olive oil

1 teaspoon salt

½ teaspoon fresh ground pepper

FOR THE DRESSING
1. Combine all the ingredients and set aside.

FOR THE SALAD
1. Prepare a charcoal or wood fire for grilling.

2. While the fire is burning down, cut the bread horizontally and brush both sides with olive oil, not too much or it will flame up and get the bread too dark which then makes the salad dark. Sprinkle with salt and pepper to taste.

3. When the fire is ready, grill the bread on both sides until lightly browned and crispy. Rub both sides of the toasted bread with the cut side of the garlic cloves to add an additional layer of flavor. Cut into the bread into ¾" cubes.

4. Add the bread cubes to a salad bowl, along with the tomatoes, green onions and basil. Toss with dressing and serve.

Serves 8-10

CHAPTER 2 • SALADS

Fiesta Slaw

This is a very popular dish that we served in the restaurant and continue to serve in the catering company. The secret is in the Cahoots Chipotle Mayonnaise. Serve with the Mexican-style baby back ribs on page 128.

SALAD
8 ounces of slaw mix, or a combination of green cabbage, red cabbage and carrots, shredded.

½ cup chopped red pepper

2 cups corn, fresh or frozen

3 green onion, thinly sliced

2 tablespoons cilantro, chopped

DRESSING
½ cup Cahoots Chipotle Mayonnaise, page 173

2 tablespoons sugar

1 tablespoon apple cider vinegar

½ teaspoon ground coriander

FOR THE SALAD
1. Combine the slaw mix, red bell pepper, corn, green onions and cilantro.

FOR THE DRESSING
2. Mix all ingredients together until sugar is dissolved. Toss with the slaw, let it rest for about 10 minutes and serve.

Serves 6-8

CAHOOTS TOO

Cahoots World Famous Thai Chicken Salad

When we had the restaurant downtown we would devote an entire day, Thursday, to this salad. It was really two days for the kitchen to prepare all the ingredients for the onslaught of customers. I have to admit we had to take the phone off the hook almost every Thursday to help manage a happy balance of restaurant customers and to-go customers. We successfully bottled the dressing but as the peanut allergy epidemic escalated we found it virtually impossible to find a co-packer to bottle it, so it's all yours!

FOR THE DRESSING
- 1 ounce garlic, about 6 cloves
- 4 chipotle peppers in adobo
- 8 ounce roasted, salted peanuts
- ⅓ cup + 1 tablespoon granulated sugar
- 1 tablespoon curry powder
- 1 tablespoon soy sauce
- 1¼ cups seasoned rice vinegar
- ⅔ cup sesame oil
- 1⅔ cups light olive oil or olive oil/canola blend

FOR THE SALAD
- 4 ounces Red cabbage, shredded
- 5 ounces Romaine lettuce, chopped
- 1 cucumber, peeled and diced
- ¼ cup cilantro leaves, coarsely chopped
- 1 bunch of green onions, chopped with some of the green tops
- 1 red bell pepper, seeded and chopped
- 5 ounces grilled chicken breast, diced

1. In the bowl of a food processor chop garlic. Add chipotle chilies and process for about 30 seconds. Add the peanuts and grind, scraping down the sides of the bowl, until well mixed, about 30 seconds.

2. With a stand mixer or hand held mixer, fitted with a whisk, transfer peanut mixture to mixing bowl. Add the sugar, curry powder, soy sauce, seasoned rice vinegar, sesame oil and olive/canola blend and mix well over medium speed.

3. In a salad bowl mix the red cabbage, romaine, cucumber, green onions, red bell peppers, cilantro and chicken. Toss with ¾-1 cup Thai salad dressing.

Serves 4-6

Chapter 2 • Salads

Chapter 3
VEGETABLES & SIDES

Roasted Yukon Gold Potatoes with Roasted Garlic & Bacon page **54**

Steamed Artichokes with Lemon Aioli page **56**

Asparagus, Goat Cheese Prosciutto Bundles page **58**

Wild Rice Salad with Snow Peas & Mushrooms page **60**

Thai Rice Salad page **61**

Roasted Brussels Sprouts with Pancetta, Dried Cranberries & Mustard page **62**

Peruvian Quinoa & Forbidden Black Rice page **64**

Mediterranean Roasted Vegetable Fritters page **66**

Black Bean, Corn & Feta page **67**

Baked Butternut Squash Risotto & Burrata with Fried Sage page **68**

Toasted Pearl Couscous & Lentils page **70**

Herbed Quinoa Pilaf with Summer Vegetables page **72**

Layered Vegetable Casserole page **73**

Cauliflower, Black Bean, Feta & Kalamata page **74**

Zucchini Brown Rice Gratin page **76**

Layered Two Potato & Fennel Gratin page **78**

Broccoli with Tomatoes, Fennel Pollen & Almonds page **80**

Roasted Fingerling Potatoes with Mustard & Garlic page **81**

Cahoots Too

Roasted Yukon Gold Potatoes
with Roasted Garlic & Bacon

I know, what is not to like here? Serve this warm or at room temperature.

2 pounds Yukon Gold potatoes, washed and cut into wedges

½ pound thick cut bacon, cut into 1" pieces

12 large cloves garlic

3 tablespoons good quality olive oil

1 teaspoon kosher salt

1 teaspoon fresh ground black pepper

1 tablespoon seasoned rice wine vinegar

1 tablespoon Dijon mustard

¼ cup good quality olive oil

1 5-ounce package baby arugula

Preheat oven to 375° F.

1. Place the potatoes, bacon, garlic olive oil, salt and pepper in a bowl and toss to coat. Spread out on a baking sheet lightly sprayed with nonstick olive oil spray and roast in the oven for 25-30 minutes, stirring once with a spatula, until golden and crispy. Transfer to a large mixing bowl, cover to keep warm.

2. In a small bowl, mix together the rice vinegar, Dijon mustard, and olive oil. Pour over the warm potato mixture and gently toss to combine. Toss in the arugula just before serving. Serve warm or at room temperature.

Serves 4-6

CHAPTER 3 • VEGETABLES & SIDES

*Serve with
Bistecca alla Cahoots
page 140*

CAHOOTS TOO

Steamed Artichokes
with Lemon Aioli

A few years ago we added steamed artichokes to our Farmers Market Vegetable Basket. I wasn't sure how they would be received, I know that I really like them but was not sure about the customer. It seems people generally like them but seem a little intimidated by them. Picking the right artichoke is crucial. Make sure the leaves are tight against the choke and that the stem is healthy and about the size of a quarter, not too small (usually not much "heart") or too large (generally a little tough).

4 artichokes, stems trimmed flush with the bottom of the choke

2 tablespoons kosher salt

1 tablespoon fresh ground black pepper

8 cloves garlic

¼ cup good quality olive oil, preferably lemon

1 shallot, peeled and thickly sliced

4 sprigs fresh rosemary

4 sprigs fresh thyme

4 sprigs fresh oregano

Lemon Aioli, page 174

1. In a large sauce pot deep enough to cover the artichokes, add 1 inch water. Stir in the salt. Add the artichokes, pepper, garlic, olive oil, shallot and fresh herbs. Bring to a boil.

2. Make the Lemon Aioli.

3. Once the water is boiling reduce the heat to low. Cover and cook for about 45 minutes or until the leaves start to pull away and are tender or use a slotted spoon, scoop up a choke and insert a knife in the bottom heart. Cook time will vary on size, freshness, and variety. Remove from heat and let sit until slightly cooled, about 10 minutes. Serve artichokes with lemon aioli or drawn butter.

Serves 4-6

CHAPTER 3 • VEGETABLES & SIDES

Serve with a Zinfandel

Cahoots Too

Asparagus, Goat Cheese Prosciutto Bundles

This was inspired by one of the wood fired pizzas that we do with all these ingredients. They are fun, can be prepared ahead of time, cook quickly, are delicious and will wow your guests.

20 asparagus spears

4 thin slices of prosciutto

1-2 tablespoons good quality olive oil

1 lemon

⅓ cup goat cheese crumbles

1 teaspoon kosher salt

1 teaspoon fresh ground black pepper

Preheat oven to 325° F.

1. Snap off tough ends of asparagus.

2. On a work surface, lay out one piece of prosciutto. Top with 5 pieces of asparagus and wrap them up in a bundle and place them seam side down on a baking sheet. Repeat with the next 3 bundles.

3. Lightly brush with olive oil. Zest the lemon over the top, then cut the lemon in half and juice the lemon onto the bundles.

4. Roast in the oven for about 10-12 minutes, the asparagus should be tender and the prosciutto crisp. Remove from the oven, sprinkle with goat cheese, salt and pepper and serve.

Serves 4

CHAPTER 3 • VEGETABLES & SIDES

Cahoots Too

Wild Rice with Snow Peas & Mushrooms

This recipe is one I have enjoyed over the years. You can serve this cold, room temp, or warm.

- 2 cups wild rice
- ¼ cup olive oil
- 4 cups vegetable stock
- ½ cup mushrooms, thinly sliced
- 1 can sliced water chestnuts
- 1 cup red bell peppers, or mix of colors, thinly sliced
- ½ cup sliced green onions
- 8 ounces snow peas, tips and strings removed, blanched for 30 seconds

DRESSING
- 2 ounces shallot, chopped
- 1 tablespoon Dijon mustard
- ¼ cup white balsamic vinager
- ¼ cup lemon juice
- 1 teaspoon salt
- ½ teaspoon fresh ground pepper
- 2 cups mild good quality olive oil

1. In a 2 quart sauce pan add olive oil over medium high heat. Add the rice and cook stirring until lightly toasted, about 1 minute. Add the stock, bring back to a boil. Reduce heat, cover and simmer until the rice is cooked and the liquid is absorbed. Let rest for 10 minutes.

2. Transfer rice to a mixing bowl. Add half of the dressing to the hot rice and stir well. Add mushrooms, water chestnuts, peppers, onion and snow peas.

3. Add the rest of the dressing, to taste, and serve. Can be served warm, room temperature or chilled.

Serves 6-8

CHAPTER 3 • VEGETABLES & SIDES

Thai Rice Salad

This is a recipe from my mother Fran, who is still trying to shake off the "Franwich" from the first cookbook. She came up with this dish using our Thai salad dressing.

1 bunch asparagus, cut into 1" pieces

8 ounces snap peas or snow peas, cut in half

2 cups cooked rice, I like a brown rice blend

8 ounces slaw mix

1 yellow bell pepper, julienned

1 red bell pepper, julienned

½ cup red onion, chopped

1 cup bean sprouts

¼ cup fresh basil, chiffonade

1 cup Thai Salad Dressing, page 50

1. Bring water to boil in a 2-quart sauce pan. Add the asparagus and cook for 30 seconds. Add the peas and cook for an additional 30 seconds. Drain and rinse under cold water

2. Combine the cooked rice, slaw mix, blanched vegetables, peppers, onion, sprouts and basil. Add dressing and toss until combined.

Serves 6-8

Cahoots Too

Roasted Brussels Sprouts
with Pancetta, Dried Cranberries & Mustard

Since Brussels sprouts are usually associated with holiday time, this makes for a great Thanksgiving or Christmas dish.

2 pounds Brussels sprouts, trimmed and halved, if large

4 ounces pancetta, chopped

2 garlic cloves, minced

1 teaspoon salt

1 teaspoon fresh ground black pepper

2 tablespoon good quality olive oil, preferably lemon

¼ cup water

2 tablespoons whole grain mustard

1 cup dried cranberries

Preheat oven to 400° F.

1. In a bowl toss together Brussels sprouts, pancetta, garlic, oil, and salt and pepper to taste, place in a 13" x 9" x 2" baking pan and spread in 1 layer.

2. Roast in upper third of oven, stirring once halfway through roasting, until sprouts are brown on edges and tender, about 20-25 minutes total.

3. Stir the mustard into the water.

4. Remove the Brussels sprouts from the oven and add the water mustard mix and the cranberries. Return to the oven for about 5 minutes more.

Serves 8-10

Cahoots Too

Peruvian Quinoa
& Forbidden Black Rice

Quinoa may be the ultimate survival food. It has everything that your body needs – fiber, vitamins, minerals, healthy fat, carbohydrates and protein. You will often hear quinoa referred to as a "grain", but quinoa is not a grain but an ancient seed that is in the same family as spinach. If you have invested in the Aji Amarillo paste for the Empanadas, page 12, here is another use for it. This dish is gluten free, vegetarian and vegan.

1 cup forbidden black rice

1 cup quinoa, use a light color such as white

½ cup green onions, chopped

2 cups fresh or frozen corn

1 poblano pepper, julienned

1 red bell pepper, julienned

1 yellow bell pepper, julienned

3 yellow wax peppers

½ cup each cilantro & parsley, chopped

DRESSING
2 garlic cloves, chopped

2 tablespoons lemon juice

⅓ cup orange juice

1 tablespoon lime juice

2 teaspoons kosher salt

¼ cup Aji Amarillo paste

¾ cup olive oil or olive canola blend

2 teaspoons orange zest

1. Bring rice and 1⅔ cups water and ½ teaspoon of salt to a boil in a large saucepan. Cover, reduce heat to low, and simmer until all liquid is absorbed and rice is tender, about 25 minutes. Remove pan from heat and let stand, covered, for 15 minutes. Spoon into a large mixing bowl to cool.

2. In another sauce pan bring 2 cups of water and ½ teaspoon of salt to a boil. Add quinoa, cover, reduce heat to low, and simmer until quinoa is tender, about 15 minutes. Drain, and add to the mixing bowl with the rice and fluff. Add the green onions, corn, peppers and herbs.

3. To make the dressing, mix all the dressing ingredients together. Pour over rice, quinoa and vegetables and serve warm, room temperature or chilled.

Serves 6-8

Chapter 3 • Vegetables & Sides

Cahoots Too

Mediterranean Roasted Vegetable Fritters

4 cloves garlic

2 cups assorted grilled vegetables, preferably eggplant, zucchini, Portobello mushroom, roughly chopped

2 cup garbanzo beans, drained

4 tablespoon flour

1 teaspoon baking powder

4 eggs, beaten

5 green onions, chopped

1 tablespoon Herbs de Provence or Italian herb mix

Salt and pepper to taste

Oil for frying

Green Olive Aioli, page 176

1. In a food processor fitted with the steel knife chop the garlic. Add the assorted vegetables, garbanzo beans, flour, baking powder, eggs, green onions, salt and pepper. Pulse, until combined but not over blended, you want to see chunks of vegetables.

2. Take a ⅓ cup measure or scoop and divide the mixture into 10-12 balls. Flatten them to about ½".

3. Heat oil in a frying pan until hot about 350° F. Cook in batches, turning once or twice, until cooked through and crispy. Drain on paper towels. Can be done ahead and reheated in the oven at 325° F for 10 minutes or serve at once with Green Olive Aioli.

Makes 10-12 fritters

CHAPTER 3 • VEGETABLES & SIDES

Black Bean, Corn & Feta

This recipe has been in our repertoire forever, and is always a favorite. Diane, one of the ladies that works with us, likes to roll this salad up in a flour tortilla and deep fry it like a flauta. Big hit!

- 3 15½-ounce cans black beans, drained and rinsed
- 8 ounces fresh or frozen corn
- 1 red bell pepper, chopped
- 5 green onions, chopped
- 2 Anaheim chiles, roasted, peeled and chopped (canned Ortega green chiles will work)
- 3 ounces (⅓ cup) feta cheese, crumbled
- ¼ cup cilantro, chopped
- 3 cloves garlic, chopped
- 1 chipotle pepper in adobo
- ⅓ cup lime juice
- 1 teaspoon cumin
- ½ tablespoon salt
- 1 tablespoon white balsamic vinegar
- ¾ cup olive oil

1. Combine the beans, corn, red bell pepper, green onion, green chiles, feta and cilantro and toss well.

2. In a food processor or blender add garlic, chipotle pepper, lime juice, cumin, salt and white balsamic vinegar. Turn on the processor and let blend for about 15 seconds. Slowly add in the olive oil and blend another 15 seconds, scraping down the side of the bowl half way through. Add to the bean mixture. Stir well and serve.

Serves 8-10

Cahoots Too

Baked Butternut Squash Risotto
& Burrata with Fried Sage

1 pound butternut squash, peeled, seeded and cut into ½" cubes

1 tablespoon olive oil

¼ cup unsalted butter

4 cloves garlic, chopped

1 small yellow onion

2 teaspoon salt

2 freshly ground pepper

1½ cups Arborio rice

¼ cup dry white wine

4 cups vegetable stock

8 ounces burrata or fresh mozzarella, chopped into ½" pieces

½ cup Parmesan cheese, grated

1 ounce fresh sage leaves

½ cup oil for frying sage leaves

Preheat the oven to 350° F.

1. Toss the butternut squash with olive oil and spread onto a baking sheet. Cook for 15 minutes or until golden. The squash will not be completely done but will finish in the risiotto. Set aside.

2. In a 4-quart sauce pan melt butter over medium heat. Add the chopped garlic and onion, cook until soft, about 3 minutes. Add the rice and stir well. Add the wine, salt and pepper, cook for about 1 minute. Add the stock and the butternut squash, stir well and pour into an 8" x 12" baking dish. Bake, uncovered, for 30-40 minutes or until the stock is almost all absorbed and the rice is al dente.

3. While the risotto is baking, warm ½ cup oil in a small frying pan. Once hot add the sage leaves and fry, turning quickly until crisp, about 30 seconds. Lightly salt.

4. Remove risotto from oven when done and stir in the burrata and Parmesan cheese. Serve garnished with fried sage leaves.

Serves 4-6

Chapter 3 • Vegetables & Sides

Toasted Pearl Couscous & Lentils

- 1 cup orange or yellow lentils
- 3 tablespoons white wine vinegar
- 1 tablespoon good quality olive oil
- 2 cloves garlic, chopped
- 1 shallot, chopped
- 1 cup pearl couscous
- 1¼ cups vegetable broth
- ½ cup fresh basil, chiffonade
- 4 ounce baby spinach
- 2 cups vine-ripened cherry tomatoes
- ¼ pound feta, crumbled (about 1 cup)
- ½ cup olive oil
- ½ cup red wine vinegar
- 2 teaspoons Dijon mustard
- 1 teaspoon salt
- 1 teaspoon fresh ground black pepper

1. In a small saucepan simmer lentils in water to cover by 2 inches until tender but not falling apart, 8 to 10 minutes, and drain well. Transfer hot lentils to a bowl and stir in 1 tablespoon vinegar and salt and pepper to taste. Cool lentils completely, stirring occasionally.

2. In a sauté pan, heat 1 tablespoon olive oil. Add the garlic and shallots and sauté for about 5 minutes. Add the couscous and cook until light golden brown, stirring often, about 5 minutes. Add the broth and bring to boil. Reduce heat to low; cover and simmer until couscous is tender and liquid is absorbed, about 10 minutes. Remove from heat and cool.

3. In a large bowl combine the lentils, couscous, basil, baby spinach, cherry tomatoes and feta cheese.

4. In a small bowl, combine the olive oil, vinegar, Dijon mustard, salt and pepper. Whisk together well and pour over the salad. Toss and serve

Serves 8-10

CHAPTER 3 • VEGETABLES & SIDES

Serve with
*Grilled Leg of Lamb with
Olive Sauce*
page 142

Cahoots Too

Herbed Quinoa Pilaf
with Summer Vegetables

1¾ cups low-salt chicken broth

½ teaspoon coarse sea salt plus additional for seasoning

1 cup quinoa

3 tablespoons olive oil

2 garlic cloves, minced

½ cup red onion, thinly sliced

1 cup yellow bell peppers, julienned

1 cup red bell peppers, julienned

½ pound asparagus, trimmed, cut on diagonal into ¾" pieces

1 cup zucchini cut in ½" dice

Kosher salt and freshly ground black pepper

4 green onions, thinly sliced

1 tablespoon chopped fresh Italian parsley

1. Bring broth and ½ teaspoon sea salt to boil in medium sauce pan; add quinoa. Cover, reduce heat to low, and simmer until quinoa is tender and broth is absorbed, about 15 minutes. Remove from heat; fluff with fork and set aside.

2. Add olive oil to a large sauté pan. Add garlic and onion, sauté 30 seconds. Add all bell peppers, asparagus, and zucchini. Sprinkle with sea salt and black pepper. Sauté, until just tender, about 6 minutes. Add cooked quinoa, green onions, and parsley to vegetables in skillet; toss to warm and combine.

Serves 4-6

CHAPTER 3 • VEGETABLES & SIDES

Layered Vegetable Casserole

- 2 eggplants, peeled, sliced into ½" pieces, lightly salt and drain
- 2 tablespoons olive oil
- 2 zucchini, sliced into ½" pieces
- ½ pound (8 ounces) mushrooms, sliced
- 2 yellow bell peppers, diced
- 3 tomatoes, sliced
- 1 5-ounce bag of baby spinach
- 2 tomatoes chopped
- 1 cup fresh grated Parmesan cheese
- ½ cup good quality olive oil
- 1 tablespoon Cahoots House Rub or other all-purpose seasoning

Preheat oven to 350° F.

1. Heat 2 tablespoons of olive oil in a frying pan over medium high heat. Working in batches lightly sauté the eggplant slices, turning once, to soften.

2. Lightly spray a 13" x 9" x 2" inch baking dish with olive oil spray. Line the bottom of the baking dish with half the eggplant in one layer. Top with half the zucchini, half the mushrooms, half yellow bell peppers, all tomato slices, and half the spinach. Drizzle with ¼ cup olive oil, 1½ teaspoons House Rub and ½ cup Parmesan cheese. Repeat the layers with the eggplant, zucchini, mushrooms, yellow bell peppers, baby spinach, chopped tomatoes, olive oil, Cahoots House Rub and Parmesan cheese.

3. Tightly cover with foil, but allow room for the foil to form a tent so it is not touching the vegetables. Bake for about 1 hour. Remove foil and serve.

Serves 10-12

Cahoots Too

Cauliflower, Black Bean, Feta
& Kalamata

1 medium head of cauliflower, trimmed, cut into small florets (about 3 cups)

1 15-ounce can black beans, drained

1 large head of radicchio, thinly sliced

2 tablespoons fresh basil, chopped

2 tablespoons fresh chives, chopped

½ cup Kalamata olives, pitted and sliced in half

½ cup crumbled feta cheese (about 3 ounces)

½ cup pine nuts lightly toasted and chopped

⅓ cup good quality olive oil

1 lemon, zested and juiced

1 tablespoon white balsamic vinegar

1½ teaspoons salt

½ teaspoon ground black pepper

1. Steam cauliflower florets until just tender (al dente) with a little bite to them.

2. Combine cauliflower, beans, radicchio, basil, chives, Kalamata olives, feta and pine nuts.

3. Whisk together olive oil, lemon zest, juice, vinegar, salt, and pepper in small bowl. Toss with the cauliflower mixture and serve.

Serves 6-8

CHAPTER 3 • VEGETABLES & SIDES

Cahoots Too

Zucchini Brown Rice Gratin

- ½ cup uncooked long grain brown rice
- ¼ cup good quality olive oil plus 1 tablespoon
- 1 medium sweet yellow onion, chopped
- 4 garlic cloves, minced
- 1½ pounds zucchini (about 3 medium), sliced ¼" thick
- ½ pound Roma tomatoes, chopped
- 2 teaspoons kosher salt
- 1 teaspoon fresh ground black pepper
- 1 tablespoon Herbs de Provence or Italian seasoning
- 2 large eggs, lightly beaten
- ½ cup grated Parmesan, divided
- ½ cup grated Fontina cheese

Preheat oven to 350° F.

1. Cook the rice according to the package directions.

2. While rice cooks, heat a large, heavy skillet over medium heat with olive oil, add onions and garlic. Sauté over medium heat until soft, about 10 minutes. Stir occasionally.

3. Add the zucchini and tomatoes and sauté for an additional 10 minutes. Remove from heat and stir in salt, pepper, and herbs.

4. Combine the cooked rice, eggs, and Parmesan in a bowl. Once combined gently stir in the sautéed vegetables.

5. Lightly coat a shallow 2-quart baking dish with 1 tablespoon olive oil. Spread the mixture into the baking dish. Top with Fontina cheese.

6. Bake, until set and golden brown, about 20 minutes.

Serves 6-8

Chapter 3 • Vegetables & Sides

Serve with a Pinot Noir

Cahoots Too

Layered Two Potato
& Fennel Gratin

This is a delicious combination of flavors, great year round but would be a good fit for the Holidays.

2 large leeks, sliced and washed

2 small fennel bulbs, cut in half, cores removed and thinly sliced

2 tablespoons unsalted butter

2 tablespoons good quality olive oil

½ pound speck ham, ¼" dice

4 cloves garlic, minced

3½ cups heavy cream

2 tablespoons fresh thyme leaves

2 teaspoons kosher salt

1 teaspoon fresh ground pepper

2½ pounds sweet potatoes, about 2 medium, peeled

2½ pounds Yukon Gold or other gold fleshed potato, no need to peel

½ pound Gruyere cheese or other good quality Swiss style cheese

Preheat oven to 350° F.

1. In a medium sauce pan over medium heat, melt the butter together with the olive oil. Add the leeks, fennel, speck ham and garlic, cook for about 5 minutes, stirring occasionally.

2. Add the cream and bring to a boil. Reduce heat and simmer for about 2-3 minutes, until it starts to thicken. Add the thyme, salt and pepper. Remove from heat and set aside.

3. Slice the sweet potatoes about ⅛" to ¼" thick, set aside. Repeat with the gold potatoes, keep them separate.

4. Butter the inside of a 13" x 9" x 2" baking dish. Arrange one layer of sweet potatoes, over lapping at the half of each slice, on the bottom of the baking dish. Repeat with a layer of the gold potatoes.

5. Spread ¾ cup of the cream mixture over the potatoes. Repeat potato layers, first sweet potatoes, then gold potatoes, and 1 cup of cream mixture. Repeat with the remaining potatoes. Pour the rest of the cream mixture over the top, spreading it evenly, submerging all potatoes. Top with cheese, cover loosely with foil and bake for about 30 minutes. Remove foil and bake for an additional 30-40 minutes. Test for doneness. Let rest for 10 minutes. Serve.

Serves 10-12

CHAPTER 3 • VEGETABLES & SIDES

CAHOOTS TOO

Broccoli with Tomatoes,
Fennel Pollen & Almonds

- 2 heads broccoli, cut into florets
- 2 cups cherry tomatoes
- ¼ cup good quality olive oil
- 2 teaspoons fennel pollen*
- 1 teaspoon Kosher salt
- 1 teaspoon fresh ground black pepper
- ½ cup sliced almonds, toasted

*www.pollenranch.com

Preheat the oven to 375° F.

1. In a medium bowl, toss the broccoli florets, cherry tomatoes, olive oil, fennel pollen, salt and pepper. Toss to coat completely. Pour onto a baking sheet in a single layer. Roast for 20 to 25 minutes, until the broccoli is tender and lightly golden brown.

2. Spoon the broccoli mixture onto warm serving platter. Sprinkle with toasted almonds. Serve immediately.

Serves 6-8

Roasted Fingerling Potatoes
with Mustard & Garlic

- 2 tablespoons extra-virgin olive oil
- 4 tablespoons butter, melted
- 2 tablespoons whole grain mustard
- 1 tablespoon Dijon mustard
- 4 cloves garlic, chopped
- 1 teaspoon coarse kosher salt
- 1 teaspoon fresh ground black pepper
- 3 pounds mixed fingerling potatoes, cut into 1" wide pieces
- 2 tablespoon fresh chives, chopped
- 2 tablespoon fresh parsley, chopped

Preheat oven to 400° F.

1. In a medium bowl, whisk together olive oil, butter, mustards, garlic, salt and pepper. Add potatoes and toss to coat. Spread potatoes in single layer on a lightly sprayed baking sheet.

2. Roast potatoes 25 minutes, stirring once half way through the cooking time, until potatoes are crusty outside and tender inside.

3. Transfer potatoes to serving bowl. Stir in fresh herbs and serve.

Serves 8-10

Chapter 4
BREADS, SANDWICHES & PASTA

Brioche Buns	page **84**
Winter Squash Loaf	page **86**
Rosemary Focaccia with Caramelized Onion	page **88**
Schiacciata	page **90**
Southwestern Chicken Melt	page **92**
BLT&P Burrata, Lettuce, Tomato and Pancetta	page **94**
Pulled Pork Slider with Fiesta Slaw	page **95**
Grilled Vegetable Wrap with Herbed Goat Cheese & Tapanade	page **96**
Cahoots Club Cobb	page **98**
Spicy Buffalo Chicken Mac & Cheese	page **100**
Lisa's Favorite Pasta, Bow Tie with Truffles	page **102**
Pasta Fresca	page **104**
Baked Rigatoni with Italian Sausage & Creamy Marinara Sauce	page **105**
Jim's Favorite Pasta, Angel Hair with Roma Tomatoes, Garlic & Basil	page **106**
Farmers Market Shirataki Noodles	page **108**
Ravioli Carbonara	page **110**

Cahoots Too

Brioche Buns

Small size for sliders and dinner rolls, large for club sandwiches and hamburgers.

- 1 cup warm water (105° F)
- ¼ cup warm milk
- 2 teaspoons active dry yeast
- 2 tablespoons sugar
- 3 cups bread flour
- 1 cup all-purpose flour
- 2 teaspoons salt
- 8 ounces unsalted butter, diced and very cold (or frozen)
- 4 large eggs
- 1 egg, whisked with ¼ cup cold water

1. In a glass measuring cup, combine 1 cup warm water, milk, yeast and sugar. Let stand until foamy, about 5 minutes.

2. In the bowl of a food processor fitted with the steel knife, add the flours, salt and butter. Process the ingredients until the butter is cut into the flour mixture.

3. Add in yeast mixture and eggs. Process until the dough forms.

4. Turn dough out onto a lightly floured surface. Shape the dough into a ball and put in a bowl (it will be sticky and wet). Cover bowl with a clean, damp kitchen towel and let the dough rise in a warm place until it has doubled in size, about 2 hours.

5. Lightly coat baking sheet with no stick spray. Using a dough scraper (or chef's knife), divide the dough into 8 equal parts (or 12 for smaller buns. Shape the dough into balls, place your palm over the top and gently roll into a smooth ball. Transfer to baking sheet, placing them 2" to 3" apart. Cover loosely with plastic wrap and let buns rise in a warm place for 1-2 hours, or until puffy and slightly risen.

6. Preheat the oven to 450° F.

7. When the buns are finished with the 2nd rise, gently brush each one with egg wash.

8. Place a shallow baking pan on the oven floor. Before the dough goes in, add about ½ cup of water to the pan (to create steam). This will help keep the bread nice and moist. Bake for about 17-20 minutes for the larger buns, 15 minutes for the small buns or until golden brown. Transfer to a wire rack to cool completely.

Makes 8 large or 12 small buns

Chapter 4 • Breads, Sandwiches & Pasta

Cahoots Too

Winter Squash Loaf

You can use any combination of winter squash such as kombucha, butternut, acorn, pumpkin for this recipe. I used butternut.

- 1 pound winter squash peeled and diced to ¼"
- ¼ cup garlic, if large cloves, cut in half
- 2 shallots, sliced
- ¼ cup olive oil
- Salt and pepper
- 2 tablespoons dry yeast
- ½ cup water, 105° F
- ½ cup olive oil
- ½ cup buttermilk
- 2 eggs, lightly beaten
- 1 tablespoon salt
- 1 tablespoon fresh sage, chopped
- 2 teaspoons sugar
- 3 cups bread flour
- ½ pound feta cheese, crumbled

Preheat oven to 375° F.

1. Toss the squash, garlic and shallots with olive oil, salt and pepper. Place on a sheet pan and roast until tender, about 20 minutes. Remove from oven and cool.

2. Put warm water in a bowl and sprinkle with yeast, stir, let stand in a warm place for about 10 minutes or until it starts to bubble.

3. In a stand mixer mixing bowl fitted with a whisk add ½ cup olive oil, buttermilk, eggs, sage, salt and sugar. Whisk until smooth. Replace the whisk with the dough hook and add the flour, squash mixture and feta. Transfer to a lightly buttered 9" x 5" loaf pan. Cover with a damp cloth and let sit in a warm place until doubled in size, about an hour.

4. Bake for 1 hour.

Serves 10-12

Chapter 4 • Breads, Sandwiches & Pasta

Cahoots Too

Rosemary Focaccia
with Caramelized Onion

Our designer's son cuts this focaccia into large squares, splits them horizontally, places the top slice onion side down onto the sandwich fillings then puts them into a panini press.

- 1 tablespoon yeast
- 2 teaspoons sugar
- 2½ cups warm milk, about 105° F
- 5 cups bread flour
- 2 teaspoons salt
- 1 teaspoon fresh ground pepper
- 20 whole cloves of garlic
- 6 shallots, sliced about ¼"
- 1 sweet yellow onion, peeled, trimmed and sliced into ¼" wedges
- ¼ cup olive oil
- 2 tablespoons sugar
- 1 tablespoon fresh rosemary leaves
- 2 tablespoons good quality olive oil

Preheat oven to 350° F.

1. Add yeast and sugar to warm milk and stir to dissolve. Put in a warm place for about 5 minutes until it starts to bubble.

2. In a stand mixer, fitted with a dough hook, add the flour, salt and pepper. Add the yeast mixture and mix until the dough forms a ball. On a lightly floured surface knead the dough until smooth and elastic adding flour to keep it from sticking, but the dough will be a little sticky when done. Place in bowl and cover with a damp towel. Let it rise in a warm place for about 30 minutes or until doubled in size.

3. While the dough is rising, toss garlic, shallots and onions with olive oil and sugar. Spread onto a sheet pan and bake until starting to caramelize, about 10-15 minutes. Remove, stir in rosemary leaves and cool.

4. Lightly oil a 17" x 12" baking sheet with olive oil. Turn dough out onto the baking sheet and gently press dough evenly onto the pan. Make several indentations on the dough with your fingers. Sprinkle with caramelized onions and garlic. Let rise for another 10 minutes.

5. Increase the oven temperature to 450° F. Place a shallow pan of water on the bottom shelf; this will create steam to help with the crispness of the crust.

6. Bake focaccia for 20 to 25 minutes until golden brown.

Serves 12-16

Chapter 4 • Breads, Sandwiches & Pasta

CAHOOTS TOO

Schiacciata (ski-ah-cha-tah)

This is a delicious Italian flatbread usually from the Tuscan region and usually on the sweet/savory side. This recipe is typically made during late summer grape harvest, but there are countless options. I think this is a great addition to brunch.

- 1½ tablespoons dry active yeast
- 2¼ cups warm water, 105° F
- 5 cups bread flour
- 1½ tablespoons salt
- ¼ cup good quality olive oil
- ½ cup unsalted butter
- ½ cup walnuts, lightly toasted and chopped
- 1 teaspoon sugar
- ½ cup red wine
- ½ cup sugar
- 2 cups seedless grapes, red and/or white
- ½ cup Gorgonzola cheese
- ½ cup blackberry or huckleberry preserves

1. Mix the yeast and warm water together and let sit until it starts to bubble.

2. In the mixing bowl of a stand mixer add the flour and salt. With the dough hook in place, turn the machine onto low and add the yeast mixture. Combine until the dough is elastic, drizzling in olive oil, 1 tablespoon at a time until smooth and elastic, about 5 minutes.

3. Place the dough in a lightly oiled bowl and turn to coat. Cover with a damp towel and let rise in a warm location until doubled in size, about an hour.

Chapter 4 • Breads, Sandwiches & Pasta

4. Punch down the dough. Turn it out on a lightly floured surface and roll into 12" x 15" rectangle. Place on an oiled sheet pan, pressing the dough to the edges to fill the pan. Cover with damp towel and let rise for 45 minutes.

Preheat oven to 425° F.

1. While the dough is proofing, melt butter in a sauté pan over medium low heat. Add the walnuts and sugar and stir until the walnuts are well coated and starting to caramelize. Let cool.

2. Heat the wine and the sugar over medium low heat until the sugar is dissolved and syrupy, about 5 minutes. Remove from heat and stir in grapes, let cool.

3. Carefully spread the preserves over the dough. Top with the grapes and drizzle with the wine syrup. Gently press the grapes into the dough. Bake for 30 minutes.

4. Remove from oven and sprinkle with caramelized walnuts and Gorgonzola, bake for an additional 15 minutes, until edges are golden brown. Let rest before slicing.

Serves 12-16

CAHOOTS TOO

Southwestern Chicken Melt

It's tough to say which sandwich was most popular in our restaurant - this one or the Cahoots Club Cobb. The secret to this sandwich is the Cahoots Chipotle Mayonnaise.

- 4 grilled chicken breasts, sliced horizontally into ¼" pieces
- 8 sliced sourdough bread
- ½-¾ cups Cahoots Chipotle Mayonnaise, page 173
- 4 roasted green chiles
- 8 slices cheddar cheese, thinly sliced
- 1 red onion, peeled and thinly sliced
- 2 tomatoes, sliced

Preheat oven broiler.

1. Heat griddle pan over medium high heat. Lightly butter or oil the griddle, add the bread, cook until nicely browned, on side only. Remove the bread and place on work surface. Add chicken to the griddle and warm through, turning once or twice. On the last turn of the chicken add the green chiles, turning once to warm through.

2. While the chicken is warming, spread the chipotle mayonnaise over the un-griddled side of the bread. Top with chicken, green chili and cheddar cheese. Place in the oven to melt the cheese, about 2 minutes. Remove from the oven and top each sandwich with onion and tomato. Place the remaining bread slices on top, slice in half and serve.

Makes 4 whole sandwiches

Chapter 4 • Breads, Sandwiches & Pasta

Cahoots Too

BLT&P
Burrata, Lettuce, Tomato & Pancetta

- 4 3-ounce packages thinly sliced pancetta (Italian bacon)
- 12 slices sourdough bread, lightly toasted
- ½ cup mayonnaise, preferably olive oil based
- 18 ounces burrata cheese or fresh mozzarella cheese
- ½ cup (packed) fresh basil, coarsely torn
- 4 cups baby arugula
- 6 vine ripe tomatoes, sliced
- Kosher salt
- Freshly ground black pepper

1. Working in batches, cook pancetta in heavy large skillet over medium heat until brown and crisp, about 6 minutes per batch. Transfer to paper towels to drain.

2. Place 6 toasted bread slices on work surface. Spread with mayonnaise. Divide the pancetta onto the bread slices. Divide the burrata among bread slices and spread to edges. Season with salt and pepper. Top each with torn basil, sliced tomatoes, and baby arugula, dividing equally. Top the other 6 slices of toasted bread with remaining mayonnaise, cover the sandwiches and press them lightly to adhere. Cut each sandwich in half and serve.

Serves 6-8

Chapter 4 • Breads, Sandwiches & Pasta

Pulled Pork Slider
with Fiesta Slaw

We have done these on many occasions either as an appetizer or as part of a slider station. If you don't want to bother with the pulled pork there are plenty of other premade options available including carnitas from your local Mexican market.

1 3- to 4-pound boneless pork shoulder, trimmed of excess fat

2 tablespoons Cahoots House Seasoning or other all-purpose seasoning

6 whole cloves garlic

2 cups vegetable stock

2 cups Cahoots Fire in the Hive Barbecue sauce or other favorite barbecue sauce

12 small brioche buns, cut in half horizontally, page 84

Fiesta Slaw, page 47

1. Cut pork shoulder into large 3" x 3" cubes. Toss with seasoning. Add pork to a slow cooker (crock pot). Add garlic and pour in vegetable stock. Cover and cook on low, 8 hours.

2. Remove pork from slow cooker. When cool enough to handle, shred the meat by hand or in batches using a food processor, pulsing to a gentle shred. Add barbecue sauce and keep warm. (Can be made ahead and rewarmed).

3. Prepare the Fiesta Slaw.

4. Warm the brioche buns in the oven or on a grill. Top each of the bottom buns with shredded pork. Top with Fiesta Slaw, cover with top bun and serve.

Serves 6-8

Cahoots Too

Grilled Vegetable Wrap
with Herbed Goat Cheese & Tapanade

2 large Portabello mushrooms, each sliced into 7 ½" slices

3 medium zucchini, sliced lengthwise into ¼" slices

2 large eggplant, peeled, sliced into ¼" slices

2 roasted bell peppers, preferably one red and one yellow, chopped

Olive oil for vegetables

Cahoots House Seasoning

4 large flour tortillas, colors are fun

1 cup Herbed Goat Cheese page 172, brought to room temperature

⅓ cup Tapenade, page 173

6 cups fresh mixed greens

1. Working in batches, toss the mushrooms and vegetables in a little olive oil to lightly coat.

2. Heat a grill pan or gas/charcoal grill to moderate heat. Grill the mushrooms and vegetables, turning once, until done, about 2 minutes a side. Season with Cahoots House Seasoning or other seasoning.

3. Warm the tortillas over a grill pan or fire to soften.

4. Place a tortilla on work surface and spread with ¼ cup herbed goat cheese, keeping the majority of the cheese in the middle leaving a 2" border on either side.

5. Spread 1 tablespoon tapenade across the center. Top with 1 ½ cups mixed greens, then 2 slices of grilled eggplant, then add 2 slices of grilled zucchini, 3 slices of Portobello mushrooms and 2 tablespoons roasted peppers.

6. Starting with the bottom edge closest to you, begin to roll pulling in the outside edges and compressing the filling to fit, it will, finishing with a sealed edge. Repeat. Cut in half on the diagonal and serve.

Serves 6-8

CHAPTER 4 • BREADS, SANDWICHES & PASTA

Cahoots Too

Cahoots Club Cobb

This sandwich was never permanently placed on the restaurant's menu, partly because it is a lot of work to make, but it was a daily special at least three days a week, and definitely worth the effort.

4 grilled chicken breasts, sliced horizontally into ¼" slices

4 Brioche buns, cut in half horizontally, page 84

8 slices thick cut, apple wood smoked bacon, cooked until crisp and drained

2 tablespoons butter

1 cup green onions

1 cup Gorgonzola cheese, crumbles

2 ripe avocados

½ cup mayonnaise

1 tomato, sliced

8 green leaf leaves

1. Heat a grill pan over medium heat. Add the sliced chicken breast slices and warm through. Remove from grill and keep warm. Add the bacon and the brioche buns, cut side down on to the grill to heat. Remove from grill and keep warm.

2. In a small sauce pan melt butter over medium heat, add green onions and sauté until soft about 2-3 minutes. Add Gorgonzola cheese and stir until melted. Keep warm.

3. Halve the avocados and remove pits. Slice each half into six to eight pieces depending on the size of the avocado.

4. To assemble, spread mayonnaise on each side of the brioche buns. On the bottom buns divide the chicken slices. Top each sandwich with 2 slices of bacon. Spoon the cheese sauce evenly over each sandwich. Top each with tomato slices and green leaf. With a large spoon, carefully scoop out the avocado and carefully fan the avocado slices into the top of the bun. Put top on, insert a toothpick or small skewer and cut in half.

Serves 4

Chapter 4 • Breads, Sandwiches & Pasta

CAHOOTS TOO

Spicy Buffalo Chicken Mac & Cheese

This recipe screams "SUPER BOWL PARTY"! This is a variation of the gourmet macaroni and cheese from the first cookbook. If you want to purchase the chicken strips already breaded that will save you a big step.

CHICKEN
- 1 pound chicken cutlets, cut into 1" strips
- 1½ cups all-purpose flour
- 2 tablespoons Cahoots House Rub or other all-purpose seasoning
- 2 eggs, beaten
- 2 cups panko bread crumbs
- Oil for frying

To eliminate this entire first process, you can purchase breaded chicken strips

- 1 cup Franks Hot Sauce®
- 1½ tablespoons cornstarch
- ¾ cup Water

MAC & CHEESE
- 4 tablespoons butter
- 2 tablespoons garlic, chopped
- ¼ cup sweet onion, chopped
- ¼ cup flour
- 3 cups whole milk
- 1 teaspoon salt
- 1 pound macaroni
- 3 quarts water
- 2 teaspoons salt
- 2 tablespoons olive oil
- 4 stalks of celery, sliced ¼"
- ½ pound sharp cheddar cheese, grated
- ½ pound Fontina cheese, grated
- ½ pound blue cheese, crumbled
- ½ cup shredded Parmesan, reserved for topping
- ¼ cup olive oil
- 1 tablespoon salt

Preheat oven to 350° F.

1. If you are breading your own chicken, mix flour and house seasoning together. In three separate bowls, one with seasoned flour, one with beaten egg and one with panko bread crumbs, start breading the chicken strips in that order.

100

CHAPTER 4 • BREADS, SANDWICHES & PASTA

2. Heat 2 inches of oil in a frying pan to about 350° F. Working in batches, add the breaded chicken and fry until golden brown. Remove and drain on paper towels. Once the chicken has drained add to a small bowl.

3. In a small sauce pan over medium heat, mix cornstarch and water together to form a slurry. Once it is hot add Franks Hot Sauce®. Stir until thickened. Pour over the chicken strips and set aside.

4. Melt butter in a 4-quart sauce pan over medium low heat. Add garlic and onions and cook slowly, stirring often until soft, about 5 minutes.

5. Add the flour and continue cooking, stirring often, for about 5 more minutes. Add milk and salt, continue cooking until it starts to come to a boil and thickens. Remove from heat.

6. Bring 4 quarts of water, 1 tablespoon of salt and ¼ cup olive oil to a boil. Add pasta and cook until al dente, about 10 minutes depending on the type of pasta you use. Drain pasta and add to a large mixing bowl.

7. Pour on the milk mixture, add the chopped celery, cheddar, Fontina and blue cheese. Mix well.

8. Butter a 13" x 9" x 2" inch baking dish or other 3 quart casserole. Spoon half the pasta mixture into the prepared dish. Top with half the chicken. Repeat with the rest of the pasta mixture, then the remaining chicken. Top with Parmesan cheese. Bake for 30 to 40 minutes, or until brown and bubbly.

Serves 12-14

Cahoots Too

Lisa's Favorite Pasta
Bowtie with Truffles

This was a lovely course that we served at Opolo Vineyards Valentines' dinner. This is so simple and elegant for any special occasion. If you have left over truffle butter, freeze it and... well the rest is easy. Serve with a crisp salad, a great bottle of wine by a roaring fire.

- 1 cup unsalted butter, softened
- 2 to 3 ounces black truffle peelings, (fresh if you can get them), try Amazon.com
- 1 large or 2 small shallots, minced
- 1½ cups cream
- 1 teaspoons salt
- 1 teaspoon fresh ground pepper
- 1 pound bowtie pasta (farfalle)
- 2 tablespoons good quality Parmesan cheese
- ¼ cup Italian flat leaf parsley, chopped

1. Combine the butter and truffle peelings together to form the truffle butter. Set aside.

2. Bring 3 quarts of water to a boil with 1 teaspoon salt and 1 tablespoon olive oil.

3. In a sauté pan over medium low heat, melt ⅔ cup truffle butter. Add the shallots and cook slowly until tender, about 4-5 minutes. Add the cream, salt and pepper and reduce until thickened.

4. While the sauce is thickening drop the pasta into the boiling water and cook as per the package instructions.

5. Drain pasta, add to the cream sauce, and toss well. Stir in 2-3 tablespoons truffle butter and Parmesan cheese and serve garnished with parsley.

Serves 4-6

Chapter 4 • Breads, Sandwiches & Pasta

Serve with an earthy Mourvèdre or Pinot Noir which would work well with the truffles (I prefer Champagne!)

Cahoots Too

Pasta Fresca

I was asked by a MOB (Mother of the Bride) to create a Tuscan-themed al fresco family style dinner for her daughter's wedding. She specifically asked for pasta fresca. This is great served warm or at room temperature and has lots of wiggle room for your own creative spin.

- ½ cup good quality olive oil
- 12 cloves garlic, chopped
- 4 shallots, chopped
- 14 fresh vine ripe tomatoes, chopped
- 1 cup pine nuts, lightly toasted
- 1 cup Kalamata olives, pitted and sliced
- 2 teaspoons salt
- 2 teaspoons fresh ground pepper
- 1 teaspoon crushed red chile flakes
- 2 cups fresh basil, chiffonade
- 1 pound pasta, preferably Penne or Fusili
- ½ cup good quality Parmesan cheese, grated

1. Bring 4 quarts of water to a boil with 1 tablespoon olive oil and 1 teaspoon salt.

2. In a large sauté pan heat olive oil over medium high heat. Add the garlic and shallots and cook for about 2 minutes. Add the tomatoes, pine nuts, Kalamata olives, salt, pepper and chili flakes. Simmer for about 8 minutes. Stir in basil, reduce heat to low and simmer until pasta is ready.

3. Add pasta to boiling water and cook for about 11 minutes, until al dente. Drain pasta and add to sauce. Stir to combine. Add to serving platter and sprinkle with Parmesan cheese.

Serves 8-10

CHAPTER 4 • BREADS, SANDWICHES & PASTA

Baked Rigatoni
with Italian Sausage & Creamy Marinara Sauce

- 1 pound rigatoni
- 1½ pounds spicy Italian sausage, casing removed
- 2 tablespoons olive oil
- 6 garlic cloves, thinly sliced
- ½ pound Crimini mushrooms, Italian brown mushrooms
- 3 cups prepared Marinara Sauce, page 170
- 1 cup mozzarella cheese, grated
- ¼ cup Parmesan cheese, grated
- 2 tablespoons fresh Italian parsley, chopped

Preheat oven to 350° F.

1. Cook rigatoni in large pot of boiling salted water until just tender but still firm to bite, stirring occasionally. Drain pasta.

2. In a large sauté pan, cook sausage over medium-high heat stirring frequently and breaking up into pieces. Drain and set aside.

3. Return pan to the stove, add olive oil. When the oil has heated add garlic and mushrooms, sauté until soft, about 2-3 minutes. Stir in marinara sauce, and bring to a simmer. Turn off the heat add the rigatoni and half the mozzarella cheese. Stir well until smooth and creamy.

4. Pour the mixture into a 13" x 9" x 2" baking dish. Sprinkle with remaining mozzarella and Parmesan.

5. Bake for about 25 to 30 minutes until cheese melts and begins to brown. Let rest for about 10 minutes. Sprinkle with parsley and serve.

Serves 6-8

Serve with a Super Tuscan blend (a big, bold blend of Italian varietals, often including Sangiovese, but not always)

CAHOOTS TOO

Jim's Favorite Pasta
Angel Hair with Roma Tomatoes, Garlic & Basil

The difference in our style of pasta dishes is a lot like our style of working together, very diverse, which makes for a good team.

- ⅔ cup good quality olive oil, Jim likes Arbequina
- 1 ounce garlic, 6-8 cloves chopped
- 2 teaspoons kosher salt
- 1 teaspoon fresh ground pepper
- ½ teaspoon crushed red pepper flakes
- 1 pound fresh Roma tomatoes, about ⅜" dice
- ½ ounce fresh basil, chiffonade most of it but reserve a few leaves for garnish
- 12 ounces angel hair pasta
- ¼ cup freshly grated Parmesan cheese

1. Bring 3 quarts of water, 1 teaspoon of salt and 1 tablespoon of olive oil to a boil.

2. In a large sauté pan add olive oil to a cold pan. Add garlic, salt and pepper and warm slowly over medium low heat, stirring occasionally.

3. When the mixture starts to simmer, add tomatoes, basil and red pepper. Heat through, about 5 minutes.

4. While the sauce is cooking, add pasta to the water and cook for about 5 minutes or until al dente. Drain. Place pasta in a bowl, add the tomato mixture and remaining basil and toss well and garnish with Parmesan cheese and fresh basil leaves.

Serves 4-6

Chapter 4 • Breads, Sandwiches & Pasta

Serve with a Dry Zinfandel (though Jim would say Bud Light!)

CAHOOTS TOO

Farmers Market Shirataki Noodles

Shirataki (shee-rah-TAH-kee) noodles are thin, low carb, gluten free, translucent traditional Japanese noodles. They are also sometimes called konnyaku noodles. They are mostly composed of a dietary fiber called glucomannan and contain very few calories and carbohydrates (sometimes even zero). Shirataki noodles are made from Konjac flour, which comes from the roots of the yam-like Konjac plant grown in Japan and China. You can find them in health food stores such as Whole Foods. This dish is vegetarian, gluten free and if you omit the cheese, vegan.

- 12 ounces Shirataki noodles (I used spaghetti-style)
- ¼ cup good quality olive oil
- 4 cloves garlic, chopped
- ½ cup red onion, thinly sliced
- ½ cup thin asparagus tips and stalks, sliced in 1" pieces
- ½ cup fresh snap peas
- ½ cup yellow bell pepper, julienned
- ½ cup red bell pepper, julianned
- ½ cup white mushrooms, thinly sliced
- 2 cups packed, fresh kale, roughly chopped
- Salt and freshly ground black pepper
- ¼ cup good quality Parmesan cheese, shaved with a vegetable peeler
- 2 tablespoons fresh chives, chopped

1. In a large pot of boiling salted water, cook the shirataki until just tender, about 2-3 minutes. Drain and set aside.

2. In a large sauté pan heat olive oil over medium heat. Add the garlic, onion, asparagus, snap peas, bell peppers, and mushrooms. Sauté the vegetables until just tender, stirring well, about 3 minutes.

3. Add the noodles and kale to the vegetables and toss well. Season with salt and pepper to taste. Spoon onto serving platter and garnish with shaved Parmesan cheese and chives.

Serves 4-6

Chapter 4 • Breads, Sandwiches & Pasta

Cahoots Too

Ravioli Carbonara

Carbonara is a pasta dish, traditionally made with spaghetti, with a sauce of cream, eggs, Parmesan cheese and bacon. I like the ravioli, it is very decadent. If you want to make your raviolis from scratch, good for you, however, there are plenty of great fresh made raviolis in many flavors available for purchase.

3 large eggs, room temperature

¾ cup freshly grated Parmesan cheese plus additional for serving

¾ cup stock, vegetable or chicken

6 slices applewood-smoked bacon, diced

3 shallots, chopped

25-30 raviolis, preferably cheese or spinach

¼ cup fresh Italian parsley, chopped

1. Whisk eggs and Parmesan in medium bowl to blend; gradually add in stock, set aside.

3. Cook bacon in large skillet over medium heat until crisp, about 8 minutes. Using slotted spoon, transfer bacon to paper towel to drain. Pour off all but about 3 tablespoons of bacon fat. Add shallots and sauté over medium heat until tender, about 6 minutes.

4. Bring water to a boil with 1 teaspoon oil and 1 teaspoon salt. Add raviolis and cook according to package, about 7-9 minutes until they start to float. Drain.

5. Add ravioli and bacon to shallot mixture in skillet and stir to heat. Turn off the heat and add the egg mixture. Stir to combine until smooth and creamy. Pour into serving dish and garnish with fresh Italian parsley and Parmesan cheese.

Serves 4-6

CHAPTER 4 • BREADS, SANDWICHES & PASTA

Serve with a Cabernet Sauvignon

Chapter 5
ENTRÉES

Ginger Wasabi Scampi
over Rice Noodles — page **114**

Halibut with Avocado
& Lemon Aioli — page **116**

Seared Sea Scallops with
Baked Lemon, Pistachio
& Vanilla Risotto — page **118**

Lemon Chicken — page **119**

Salmon Wellington
with Fresh Herb Pesto — page **120**

Fish Tacos — page **122**

Jerk Spiced Mixed Grill Kebobs — page **124**

Chicken & Eggplant Parmesan — page **126**

Costillas Adobado (Grilled Mexican
Style Baby Back Ribs)
with Grilled Pineapple Salsa — page **128**

Sweet and Sour Pork Loin
with Tomato & Cipollini Onions — page **131**

Southwestern Chicken Lasagna — page **132**

Chicken Provençal
with Green Olive Aioli
& Mediterranean Fritters — page **134**

Bacon Wrapped Pork Loin
with Pomodoro Chimichurri — page **136**

Simple Stir-Fry — page **138**

Carne Asada (Grilled Skirt Steak) — page **139**

Bistecca alla Cahoots — page **140**

Grilled Leg of Lamb
with Olive Sauce — page **142**

George Munger's Steak au Poivre — page **143**

Short Ribs — page **144**

Photo by Mollie Jane Photography

CAHOOTS TOO

Ginger Wasabi Scampi
over Rice Noodles

- 9- to 10-ounce package Chinese noodles, udon noodles or soba noodles
- ⅓ cup good quality olive oil
- 2 pounds raw shrimp, peeled and deveined (16-20 pieces per pound)
- 6 cloves garlic, chopped
- 1 tablespoon fresh ginger root, peeled and finely chopped
- 2-3 teaspoons wasabi paste (to your taste)
- ¾ cup dry white wine
- 8 tablespoon or 1 stick of butter, cut into 8 pieces
- 2 teaspoons salt
- ½ cup fresh cilantro, chopped

1. Prepare the water for your noodles, and bring it to a boil. Cook noodles according to package directions.

2. Heat olive oil in a large sauté pan over medium high heat. Add the shrimp and sauté for about 2 minutes or until almost done. Remove shrimp from pan with a slotted spoon into a bowl and keep warm.

3. Add the garlic, ginger, wasabi paste and wine. Cook over high heat for about a minute stirring occasionally. Add the butter and the salt to the sauté pan and cook until melted. Stir in the shrimp, stir well, remove from heat.

4. Stir in noodles. Toss the noodles with the shrimp. Pour noodles and shrimp onto a large serving platter. Sprinkle cilantro, and serve.

Serves 6-8

Chapter 5 • Entrées

Serve with a Viognier or a dry Riesling

Cahoots Too

Halibut with Avocado
& Lemon Aioli

In my opinion, halibut and avocado is a match made in heaven. This is easy to prepare and presents beautifully.

8 6-ounce halibut fillets

Cahoots House Rub

2-3 ripe avocados

Lemon Aioli, page 174

Preheat oven to 400° F.

1. Season the halibut with Cahoots House Rub

2. Make the Lemon Aioli.

3. Halve the avocados and remove pits. Slice each half into six to eight pieces depending on the size of the avocado. With a large spoon, carefully scoop out the avocado and top each piece of fish with a fan of about five to seven pieces. Top with a generous dollop of aioli.

4. Bake until the fish is just barely done and the aioli is beginning to brown, about seven minutes.

Serves 8

CHAPTER 5 • ENTRÉES

*Serve with
a rich, oaky Chardonnay*

CAHOOTS TOO

Seared Sea Scallops
with Baked Lemon, Pistachio & Vanilla Risotto

Although this breaks with tradition, you can bake your risotto. Saves you a lot of time and you can work on the scallops while the risotto is baking.

RISOTTO
¼ cup unsalted butter

1 small yellow onion, chopped

½ vanilla bean, split

1 teaspoon salt

1½ cups Arborio rice

¼ cup dry white wine

4 cups vegetable stock

1 cup Parmesan cheese, grated

1 tablespoon lemon zest

½ cup pistachios, lightly toasted, coarsely chopped

SCALLOPS
¼ cup good quality olive oil, lemon infused would be great

2 pounds 15-18 count sea scallops, seasoned with salt and pepper

1 cup micro parsley or ½ cup Italian flat leaf parsley, roughly chopped

Preheat oven to 350° F.

FOR THE RISOTTO
1. In a 4-quart sauce pan melt butter over medium heat. Add the chopped onion and cook until soft, about 3 minutes. Add the vanilla bean, salt, rice and wine and cook for about 1 minute. Add the stock, stir well and pour into a 8" x 12" baking dish. Bake, uncovered, for 30-40 minutes or until the stock is almost all absorbed and the rice is al dente.

2. Remove the vanilla bean. Stir in the Parmesan cheese, lemon zest and pistachios. Cover and keep warm.

FOR THE SCALLOPS
1. In a large frying pan heat olive oil over high heat. Sear scallops, about 2 minutes per side, until opaque part way through for medium.

2. To serve, divide the risotto into serving bowls. Divide the scallops into each bowl, sprinkle with parsley.

Serves 6-8

CHAPTER 5 • ENTRÉES

Lemon Chicken

This is simple and quick. You can substitute orange in place of the lemon for a little variety. This is great served with the Wild Rice Salad with Snow Peas and Mushrooms, page 60.

- 4 chicken breasts, boneless and skinless, about 1½ pounds
- ¼ cup lemon juice
- ½ cup all-purpose flour
- 2 teaspoons kosher salt
- 1 teaspoon paprika
- ½ teaspoon fresh ground pepper
- ¼ cup + 2 tablespoons good quality olive oil, divided
- 3 tablespoons, garlic, about 10 cloves, minced
- ⅓ cup dry white wine
- 2 lemons, zested and then juiced
- 3 tablespoons brown sugar
- 1 teaspoon fresh thyme leaves, lightly chopped
- Kosher salt and freshly ground black pepper
- 1 lemon, sliced crosswise

Preheat the oven to 400° F.

1. Place chicken breasts in a medium bowl. Toss with ¼ cup lemon juice, let marinate 30 minutes.

2. Drain chicken and pat dry with paper towels. Put the flour, salt, paprika, and pepper in a large resealable plastic bag and mix well. Add the chicken to the bag, shake and coat well.

3. Heat ¼ cup olive oil in a skillet over medium high heat. Add the chicken and cook until crispy and lightly browned, this will finish in the oven. Let rest on paper towels.

4. Wipe out the skillet and return to the stove. Add the remaining 2 tablespoons of olive oil. Add the garlic cook for about 1 minute. Remove from heat, add the white wine, lemon zest, lemon juice, brown sugar, thyme, salt and ½ teaspoon black pepper and pour into a 9" x 12" baking dish.

5. Place the chicken breasts over the sauce.

6. Bake for 20-25 minutes, chicken is golden brown and crisp. Serve hot with the pan juices. Garnish with the lemon slices

Serves 4

Salmon Wellington
with Fresh Herb Pesto

FRESH HERB PESTO
2 cloves garlic

2 cups fresh basil leaves (lightly packed)

½ cup fresh parsley, (lightly packed)

¼ cup fresh tarragon leaves

2 tablespoons fresh dill

½ cup pine nuts

½ cup Parmesan cheese, grated

1 lemon, zested and juiced

½ cup good quality olive oil

1 teaspoon salt

½ teaspoon fresh ground black pepper

SALMON WELLINGTON
1 pkg store bought puff pastry sheets, defrosted, unwrapped and unfolded (cover with damp towel and keep cold until ready to use)

6 6- to 7-ounce salmon fillets, skin off, pin bones removed

Cahoots House Rub or other all-purpose seasoning

Egg wash

Preheat oven to 400° F.

FOR THE PESTO,
1. Add the garlic cloves to a food processor and chop. Add the fresh herbs, pine nuts, Parmesan cheese, lemon zest and juice. With the motor running, slowly add the olive oil, scraping down the sides of the work bowl once or twice. Season with salt and pepper. Can be made a day ahead, covered and refrigerated.

FOR THE SALMON WELLINGTON,
1. Cut pastry sheet into 3 strips, you can use the fold lines as a guide, then cut each strip in half. Lay the sheets of pastry lengthwise on a lightly floured work surface. Season each salmon fillet with rub. Spread 1 tablespoon of herb pesto onto each fillet. Starting at the top of pastry closest to you gently roll out the pastry to fit the fillet, about 4" x 6". Set salmon horizontally on end of pastry. Gently roll the fish up in the pastry and place seam side down, pesto side up on a lightly greased baking sheet. Brush with egg wash.

2. Bake for about 15 minutes until puffy and golden brown. Place onto serving platter and serve with fresh herb pesto.

Serves 6

CHAPTER 5 • ENTRÉES

Serve with a Pinot Noir (Red Wine? Yes! Forget the traditional white wine with fish here; salmon and pinot are a perfect match.)

CAHOOTS TOO

Fish Tacos

I love these traditional Baja-style fish tacos. The other, healthier version is a warm corn tortilla, grilled halibut fillet and Greek yogurt version of tartar sauce. Fortunately or unfortunately, the second one is much easier to make.

BEER BATTER

1½ cups all-purpose flour

½ cup cornstarch

2 teaspoons Cahoots House Rub or other seasoning

1 teaspoon baking powder

12-ounce bottle of beer, preferably dark

FISH TACOS

2 pounds fresh halibut, cod or mahi mahi

Oil for frying

1 cup all-purpose flour

2 teaspoons Cahoots House Rub or other seasoning

8 corn tortillas, fried almost to crisp or warm them on the grill when you cook the fish

2 cups Jack and cheddar cheese blend, grated

2 cups red cabbage, finely shredded

Tartar sauce, page 175

Pico de gallo, page 176

Hot Sauce

FOR THE BEER BATTER

1. Add the first four ingredients to a bowl and mix well. Gradually whisk in the beer. If too thick, thin with a little more beer or water. Set aside until ready to use, but not longer than 20 minutes.

FOR THE TACOS

1. Trim the fish into 1" x 5" pieces.

2. Mix the flour and Cahoots House Rub together in a small bowl for dredging.

3. Heat about two inches of oil in a frying pan to 350°. Working in batches, dredge each piece of fish into the flour mixture, then into the beer batter and fry until golden brown, about 4 minutes. Drain on paper towel, lightly salt and keep warm until ready to assemble.

4. To assemble tacos, add one piece of fish to each tortilla, spoon on two to three tablespoons tartar sauce, add shredded cheese and top with cabbage. Serve with pico de gallo and your favorite hot sauce.

Serves 4-6

Chapter 5 • Entrées

These beg for beer, even a hoppy IPA, but a dry Roussanne would work as well.

Cahoots Too

Jerk Spiced Mixed Grill Kebobs

This is a popular item on our catering menu. It offers a good selection of ingredients and is a beautiful presentation. We served these at our wedding reception (that we catered, never do that) over Wine Festival Weekend (never do that either). It is important to get the portion amounts close as you will need all the meats to cook together and still finish with the appropriate doneness. Ask your butcher to help with portioning to make life easier.

KEBOBS
2 pounds beef tenderloin, trimmed and portioned into 3 ounce portions, in a bowl

1½ pounds pork tenderloin, trimmed and portioned into 2½ ounce portions, in a bowl

1½ pounds chicken breast, trimmed and portioned into 2 ounce portions, in a bowl

2 red bell peppers, cut in half, seeded and deveined, cut in 1½" squares

2 yellow bell peppers, same as above

2 green bell peppers, same as above

3 large red onions, trimmed, peeled and quartered

½ pound sausage (your preference, I like kielbasa), sliced into ¾" pieces

10 10-12" heavy duty wooden or metal skewers (if wooden, soak in water for about 15 minutes before loading to prevent burning)

JERK MARINADE
8 cloves garlic, chopped

1 cup olive oil

½ cup Jerk seasoning

¼ cup balsamic vinegar

Chapter 5 • Entrées

1. Make the marinade by whisking together garlic, olive oil, jerk seasoning and balsamic vinegar.

2. Re-whisk the marinade and divide it over the three meats for an even distribution of marinade, stir well, cover and marinate 6 to 8 hours or overnight.

3. Arrange all your ingredients in separate bowls, remove the meat from the refrigerator and stir well.

4. Start loading your skewers. First is the pork tenderloin, next a piece of onion, next a piece of red bell pepper, next a piece of beef tenderloin, next a piece of red onion, next a piece of yellow bell pepper, next a piece of chicken breast, next a piece of red onion, next a piece of green bell pepper, next a piece of sausage. Be careful not to crowd the meats, keeping in mind you want the chicken cooked, the pork medium (or more) and the beef medium rare.

5. Prepare the grill. Grill until meats are done and vegetables have a nice char to them.

Serves 8-10

Cahoots Too
Chicken & Eggplant Parmesan

This is the best of both worlds. Two great dishes made into one.

2½ cups fresh sourdough bread crumbs, lightly toasted

½ cup Parmesan cheese, grated

2 tablespoons Italian seasoning

2 large eggplant, peeled, sliced crosswise into half inch thick round pieces

2 pounds boneless, skinless chicken breasts or thighs, pounded thin, about ¼"

8 eggs, whisked

2 cups flour seasoned with 2 tablespoons Cahoots House Rub

Olive oil for frying

6 cups Marinara Sauce, page 170

1 cup Parmesan cheese, divided

3 cups mozzarella, grated

Preheat oven to 350° F.

Lightly spray or grease a 13" x 9" x 3" baking dish.

1. Mix the lightly toasted bread crumbs, Parmesan cheese and Italian seasoning together.

2. One at a time, dredge the eggplant into the seasoned flour, shaking off extra, then dip into the egg mixture and then into the bread crumb mixture, coating both sides.

3. Repeat with chicken.

4. Heat oil over medium high heat. Working in batches, fry the eggplant until golden brown, turning once. Starting with a clean pan and clean oil repeat with the chicken. The chicken will be a little under done, but it will finish in the oven. Drain on paper towels and season them both with salt and pepper.

5. To assemble, spread one cup of marinara sauce to the bottom of the baking dish, top with half the eggplant, then half the chicken in layers. Spread an additional three cups marinara over the chicken. Sprinkle ½ cup Parmesan over the marinara. Repeat with a layer of eggplant, a layer of chicken, two cups marinara and Parmesan cheese. Top with mozzarella. Bake uncovered for 1 hour.

Serves 10-12

CHAPTER 5 • ENTRÉES

Serve with a Chianti

Costillas Adobado
(Grilled Mexican-Style Baby Back Ribs) with Grilled Pineapple Salsa

This is a great do-ahead recipe that can be finished in the oven the next day. The Spanish term adobado refers to a dish that has been marinated and that generally contains chiles. In this dish I use ancho chiles. You have to cut them in half and seed them.

RIBS
3 racks baby back ribs

Cahoots House Rub or other favorite all-purpose rub

ADOBADO
1 cup pineapple juice

2 ounces dried ancho/pasilla peppers, seeded, deveined and coarsely chopped

10 whole cloves garlic

1 small onion, cut into 6-8 pieces

1½ cups crushed tomatillos

1 tablespoon beef base (I like Better than Bouillon)

2 tablespoons brown sugar

3 tablespoons lime juice

1 teaspoon salt

¼ cup sesame seeds

1 bunch cilantro

SALSA
2 cloves garlic

2 jalapeño peppers, grilled, skins removed, seeding and deveining optional (I leave mine whole)

1 pineapple, grilled, rind removed, cored and cubed

¼ cup lime juice

½ bunch fresh cilantro, chopped

1 teaspoon agave syrup

1 teaspoon salt

Prepare a charcoal or wood fire to pre-cook the ribs, grill the pineapple and the jalapeños

1. Generously season the ribs, set aside.

2. Cut pineapple in 5 1" thick slices. When the fire is ready, grill the ribs, turning occasionally until the bones start to bleed. The ribs will not be completely cooked but should have good color and smoke and will finish in the oven.

3. While the ribs are cooking grill the pineapple slices, turning once, until lightly golden. Grill the jalapeños until the skins start to darken and blister. Put in a small plastic bag and steam for about 15 minutes. Put the ribs on a baking sheet and cool slightly.

Continued on page 130

Chapter 5 • Entrées

Serve with a Garnacha (the Spanish equivalent of Grenache)

Costillas Adobado
(Grilled Mexican-Style Baby Back Ribs) with Grilled Pineapple Salsa - continued

FOR THE ADOBADO

1. Heat the pineapple juice in a small, non-reactive sauce pan until it starts to simmer. Add the ancho chiles and let simmer for about 1 minute. Turn off the heat, cover and let steep for about 5 minutes.

2. In food processor fitted with the steel blade or blender add garlic, onion, tomatillos, beef base, brown sugar, lime juice, salt, sesame seeds and cilantro. Add the chiles and pineapple juice. Blend until smooth.

3. Using a brush or your hands, coat the underside of the ribs with the adobado. Flip them over and generously coat the top of the ribs with remaining adobado. Refrigerate overnight.

Preheat oven to 300° F.

1. To finish the ribs put in the oven for 3 hours. Cut and serve with Grilled Pineapple Salsa.

FOR THE SALSA

1. In a food processor fitted with the steel blade add the garlic and chop. Add the jalapeños, grilled pineapple, lime juice, cilantro, agave syrup and salt. Process until smooth. Pour into a small sauce pan and warm over low heat.

Serves 6-8

CHAPTER 5 • ENTRÉES

Sweet and Sour Pork Loin
with Tomato & Cipollini Onions

½ cup brandy

⅓ cup golden raisins

6 center cut boneless pork loin steaks, 1" thick

Cahoots House Seasoning

2 tablespoons olive oil

1½ pounds Cipollini onions, peeled

1 tablespoon sugar

1 16-ounce can fire-roasted tomatoes with juice

2 tablespoons balsamic vinegar

1 teaspoon salt

1 teaspoon fresh thyme leaves

½ teaspoon fresh ground black pepper

Preheat oven to 325° F.

1. In a small sauce pan, over low heat, bring the brandy to a simmer. Remove from heat and add the raisins, set aside.

2. Season the pork loin on both sides with the Cahoots House Seasoning. Heat the oil in a large sauté pan over medium high heat. Brown the pork, turning once, about 3 minutes a side. Transfer to a baking dish.

3. Add the onions to the pan and cook, stirring frequently, until they start to brown. Add sugar, stir about a minute more. Add the tomatoes with juice, vinegar, spices and brandy raisin mixture. Bring to a boil, remove from heat and pour over the pork. Cover tightly with foil. Bake for 2 hours.

Serves 6

Cahoots Too

Southwestern Chicken Lasagna

This is a spin on our traditional lasagna that we have been serving our customers for the past twenty three years. This is great served with Lisa's Favorite or Jim's Favorite Salad.

TOMATILLO SAUCE
1 tablespoon olive oil

3 cloves garlic, minced

3 chipotle peppers in adobo, minced

12 ounces onion, chopped

2 27-ounce cans crushed tomatillos

1 teaspoon sugar

2 teaspoons salt

1 teaspoon ground cumin

1 teaspoon dried oregano

9 ounces lasagna noodles, uncooked, about 8

½ pound Jack/cheddar cheese blend, shredded

1½ pounds chicken, cooked and shredded

RICOTTA FILLING
1½ pounds ricotta cheese

¼ cup black olives, sliced

10 ounces fire roasted corn and peppers, canned, frozen or fresh

¼ cup cilantro, chopped

1½ cups Jack/cheddar cheese blend, shredded

1 egg

2 teaspoons salt

1 teaspoon ground cumin

1 teaspoon dried oregano

FOR THE TOMATILLO SAUCE
1. In a non reactive sauce pan add the olive oil and heat over medium heat. Add the garlic, chipotle and onions and sauté, stirring occasionally, until soft, about 5 minutes. Add the tomatillos and spices. Reduce heat and simmer uncovered for about 30 minutes.

FOR THE RICOTTA FILLING
1. In a bowl combine filling ingredients and mix well.

TO ASSEMBLE THE LASAGNA
Preheat oven to 350° F

1. In a 13" x 9" deep walled baking dish, spread 1 cup of the tomatillo sauce. Top with half the noodles. Spread 2 cups tomatillo sauce over the noodles. Divide the Ricotta mixture in half. Scatter one half over the sauced noodles. Top with half the shredded chicken.

2. Repeat layers beginning with noodles, 2 cups tomatillo sauce, the rest of the ricotta mixture, and shredded chicken.

3. Top with ½ cup of grated Jack/cheddar cheese. Cover with aluminum foil, wrap tightly and bake for 1 hour and 30 minutes. Allow lasagna to stand for about 10 minutes before serving.

Serves 10-12

Chapter 5 • Entrées

Serve with a dry Zinfandel or dry Syrah

133

Chicken Provençal
with Green Olive Aioli & Mediterranean Fritters

Mediterranean Fritters can be made ahead and reheated while you finish the chicken.

- 8 chicken breasts, skin and wing joint on
- 1 cup olive oil
- 1 tablespoon garlic, chopped
- 1 tablespoon kosher salt
- 2 tablespoons Herbs de Provence
- Black and green olives, sliced
- Green Olive Aioli, page 176
- Mediterranean Fritters, page 66

Preheat oven to 400° F.

1. Mix together the garlic, salt, 1 tablespoon Herbs de Provence and olive oil together. Add the chicken breasts, coat well with marinade and refrigerate for about 4 hours.

2. While the chicken is marinating, make the Green Olive Aioli and the Mediterranean Fritters.

3. Remove the chicken from the marinade and place onto a cooking sheet, wing up. Sprinkle with the remaining 1 tablespoon of Herbs de Provence. Bake for 30-40 minutes until crispy and golden brown.

4. Serve topped with the Green Olive Aioli, Mediterranean Fritters and garnish with some additional chopped green and black olives.

Serves 8

Chapter 5 • Entrées

Serve with a Sauvignon Blanc or Marsanne

Cahoots Too

Bacon Wrapped Pork Loin
with Pomodoro Chimichurri

Pork loin is notorious for being somewhat dry and boring, not here. This is a new addition to our catering menu and it has been a big hit. Pomodoro, an Italian word for tomato, and chimichurri, a thick Argentinian herb sauce come together in this delightful combination. If you can find Pomodoraccio, an Italian semi sun-dried tomato, that works best.

- 1 4-pound pork loin
- 1 pound thick cut bacon, about 15 pieces

BRINING LIQUID
- 8 cups very hot water
- ½ cup kosher salt
- ¼ cup brown sugar
- 1 tablespoon course ground pepper
- 2 bay leaves

POMODORO CHIMICHURRI SAUCE
- 6 garlic cloves
- 1 large shallot
- 1 jalapeño, or other favorite chile
- 2 cups fresh flat leaf parsley
- 1 cup fresh cilantro leaves
- ¼ cup fresh oregano or sweet marjoram leaves
- 1 cup Pomodoraccio or sun-dried tomatoes in oil, drained and coarsely chopped
- 2 teaspoons kosher salt
- ½ cup red wine vinegar
- 1 cup good quality olive oil

FOR THE BRINE
1. Mix all brining ingredients together and stir until salt and sugar are dissolved. Pour into a 4 quart stainless steel bowl, let cool.
2. Place the pork loin in the cooled brine, submerging completely. Let marinate for 12-24 hours in the refrigerator.

FOR THE CHIMICHURRI
1. Add the garlic, shallot and pepper to the bowl of a food processor and chop. Add the fresh herbs, tomatoes, salt and vinegar. Pulse the machine while slowly adding in the oil until blended.

Preheat oven to 350° F.

1. Remove pork loin from the brine and pat dry. Place in a roasting pan. Lay bacon slices crosswise over the roast, slightly overlapping with the ends tucked in underneath the roast.
2. Bake for about 1 hour or until the internal temperature is 140° F. Remove from oven, tent with foil and let rest for about 15 minutes.
3. Slice into 1" slices. Arrange on a serving platter. Drizzle with pomodoro chimichurri sauce.

Serves 8-10

CHAPTER 5 • ENTRÉES

Cahoots Too

Simple Stir-Fry

Jim and I love Chinese food, I usually make it for him on special occasions, but it can be a lot of work. Once you get a feel for the ingredients that you like, you can come up with personal formulas to simplify the process that will best fit your taste. This is one of mine.

KUNG PAO BROCCOLI CHICKEN

⅓ cup chicken stock

¼ cup soy sauce, preferably low sodium

2 tablespoons cornstarch

¼ cup water

1 teaspoon ground ginger

2 tablespoons vegetable oil

1 pound chicken breast, sliced in ¼" slices

3 cloves garlic, minced

½ cup onion, chopped

¼ cup celery, sliced

2 cups broccoli florets

⅓ cup red bell peppers, julienned

¼ cup peanuts

6-8 hot dried chiles, (I like chili de Arbol or chili Japones)

1. In a small bowl, mix together, stock, cornstarch, water and ginger.

2. In a wok or large frying pan, heat 2 tablespoons oil over high heat. When hot add the chicken, stirring quickly, for about 1 minute. Add the vegetables and cook, stirring quickly for another minute or two. Add the liquid, stirring well until the mixture begins to thicken. Add the peanuts and the chiles. Transfer to a serving bowl and serve with hot white or brown rice or noodles,

Serves 4-6

THE FORMULA
Here is the basic "formula" with some ingredient ideas, feel free to use any of your favorites.

1 pound protein (chicken, beef, pork, shrimp, duck, turkey, tofu)
3 cups assorted vegetables (onion, garlic, celery. Bell peppers, snap peas, bok choy, zucchini, broccoli, Napa cabbage, etc.)
¼ cup nuts (peanuts, cashews, slivered almonds, sesame seeds, etc.)
⅓ cup stock (beef, chicken, vegetable)
¼ cup soy sauce, preferably low sodium
2 tablespoons cornstarch
¼ cup water
1 teaspoon ground ginger

CHAPTER 5 • ENTRÉES

Carne Asada (Grilled Skirt Steak)

The trick here is to try to get choice or better grade of meat (prime is amazing) for this dish. This will serve a crowd. I suggest a green salad (such as, Jim's Favorite Salad recipe page 47), rice, beans, lots of fresh tortillas and a salsa bar.

4- to 5-pound choice skirt steak, prime if you can get it

8 cloves garlic

1 tablespoon fresh rosemary leaves

1 tablespoon fresh thyme leaves

1 tablespoon fresh oregano leaves

¼ cup fresh lime juice

¼ cup fresh pineapple juice

2 tablespoons seasoned rice wine vinegar

1 tablespoon salt

2 teaspoon fresh ground black pepper

¾ cup olive oil/canola blend

Corn and flour tortillas

Salsa

1. In the food processor add the garlic and chop. Add the rosemary, thyme, oregano, lime juice, pineapple juice, vinegar, salt and pepper. With the motor running chop ingredients together. Slowly add the oil and blend about 30 seconds.

2. Place skirt steak in a shallow glass baking dish. Top with marinade and coat well. Marinate for 6-8 hours.

Prepare a charcoal or wood fired barbecue.

3. Grill the skirt steak over hot coals until desired doneness, about 4 minutes a side for medium. Slice against the grain and serve with fresh corn and flour tortillas and salsa.

Serves 10-12

139

Bistecca alla Cahoots

This is my version of Bistecca alla Fiorentina, a classic Italian steak dish traditionally marinated and or basted with rosemary and olive oil; it is traditionally served very rare with cannellini beans and lemon wedges. I call dibs on the filet!

- 2 1½" thick Porterhouse steaks, about 4 pounds
- 4 cloves garlic
- ¼ cup fresh rosemary leaves
- 1 teaspoon kosher salt
- 1 teaspoon fresh ground pepper
- 1 teaspoon ground coriander
- 1 teaspoon Dijon mustard
- 1 lemon, zested and juiced
- 1 tablespoon balsamic vinegar
- ½ cup olive oil
- Cahoots House Rub

1. Add the garlic to the bowl of a food processor fitted with the steel knife. and chop. Add the rosemary, salt, pepper, coriander, Dijon, lemon zest, juice and vinegar. With the motor running slowly add the olive oil and blend until smooth, about 1 minute. The marinade will be thick.

2. Lightly season both sides of each steak with Cahoots House Rub. Place in a shallow dish and generously massage on the marinade to all sides. Marinate 6-8 hours or overnight.

Prepare charcoal or wood fired barbecue.

3. Grill steaks over coals, flipping once, about 5 minutes per side for very rare, 7-9 minutes per side for medium rare. Let steak rest, covered with foil for about 5 minutes. Cut the steak off the bone and slice against the grain.

Serves 4

CHAPTER 5 • ENTRÉES

Serve with a Cabernet Sauvignon

Cahoots Too

Grilled Leg of Lamb with Olive Sauce

1 well-trimmed 6-pound boneless leg of lamb, butterflied to even 2" thickness

4 cloves garlic, chopped

2 tablespoons Dijon mustard

Zest and juice of 1 orange

Zest and juice of 1 lemon

½ cup fresh mint chopped

½ cup fresh rosemary, chopped

½ cup red wine

¼ cup soy sauce

¼ cup balsamic vinegar

¼ cup brandy

½ cup extra-virgin olive oil

1 tablespoon fresh ground black pepper

1 tablespoon Cahoots House Rub

OLIVE SAUCE
Tapenade, page 173

½ cup of good quality olive oil

1 tablespoon fresh rosemary chopped

1 tablespoon fresh mint chopped

1. Combine garlic, mustard, orange zest and juice, lemon zest and juice, herbs, wine, soy sauce, balsamic, brandy, olive oil, and spices in the food processor. Blend until coarse puree forms.

2. Lay the lamb out on a large glass baking pan. Spread underside of lamb with half of puree. Flip the lamb and spread remaining puree over top of lamb. Cover lamb with plastic wrap and chill overnight.

3. Combine all ingredients for Olive Sauce in a food processor, Pulse to combine.

3. Let lamb stand at room temperature for about 1 hour. Prepare barbecue (medium-high heat). Grill lamb to desired doneness, about 17 minutes per side for medium-rare. Transfer lamb to cutting board; let rest 10 to 20 minutes. Carve the lamb against the grain. Serve slices slightly over lapping drizzled with the Olive Sauce.

Serves 6-8

CHAPTER 5 • ENTRÉES

George Munger's Steak au Poivre

George and Piret Munger are my mentors. George, a fabulous chef, and his wife Piret, a publicist and author of Piret's Cookbook, *welcomed me into their culinary world when I was the ripe old age of 18 and it was an amazing journey. To this day I am reminded and cherish the time I spent working for them, it still seems like yesterday. This is a signature dish of theirs.*

HERB BUTTER
1 tablespoon fresh parsley, chopped

1 tablespoon fresh chive, chopped

4 tablespoons butter, room tempurature

4 drops Tabasco® sauce

2 teaspoons Worcestershire sauce

2 lemons, juiced

1 cup Cognac

STEAKS
4 1½" thick, beef tenderloin steaks, trimmed, preferably choice or better

Whole peppercorns, I like to use the mixed peppercorns

2 tablespoons Kosher salt

FOR THE HERB BUTTER
1. Mix all the ingredients together. Divide into portioned disks and chill until ready to use.

FOR THE STEAKS
1. Coarsely crush the peppercorns in a mortar and pestle or spice grinder. Press the peppercorns into both sides of the steak until nicely crusted. Allow the crusted steak to sit for 30 minutes.

2. Heat a large cast iron skillet over high heat and sprinkle with salt. When the salt begins to "jump" in the pan, add the steaks and sear for about 1½ to 2 minutes. Turn the steak and top with the butter disks. Sear for a minute longer. Turn down the heat and carefully add the Cognac, if it does not light on its own then ignite it with a long match. When the flames have subsided, turn off heat and let steaks rest for about 3 minutes.

Serves 4

Cahoots Too

Short Ribs

Yes probably one of my personal favorites when done right. I have experimented with many different variations over the years, but this is the one we come back to time and time again. Remember to make extra so you will have leftovers for the Empanadas (page 12) they freeze well. I like to make these a day or two ahead and reheat them.

- 5 pounds boneless short ribs*
- Cahoots House Rub or other all-purpose seasoning
- ½ cup all-purpose flour
- 4 tablespoons olive oil
- 6 cloves garlic, chopped
- 2 sweet yellow onions, chopped
- 2 ribs celery, coarsely chopped
- 2 carrots, coarsely chopped
- 3 tablespoons Herbs de Provence
- 2 cups good red wine
- 2 cups beef stock
- 1 15-ounce can whole peeled tomatoes in juice
- ¾ cup balsamic vinegar
- 2 tablespoons corn starch

Preheat oven to 300° F.

1. Portion out your short ribs into 8 portions. Season with Cahoots House Rub and then dredge in flour, shake off excess.

2. Heat 2 tablespoons of olive oil in a sauté pan over medium high heat. Brown the short ribs in batches on all sides, about 6 minutes. Remove from pan and put into a baking dish, discard the oil and burnt particles from the sauté pan.

3. Add the remaining 2 tablespoons of olive oil to the pan over medium high heat. Add garlic, onions, celery, carrots, and Herbs de Provence and cook, stirring often until vegetables are soft, about 6-8 minutes. Add wine and reduce by half, add beef stock, tomatoes with juice and vinegar, simmer for about 2 minutes. Pour the mixture over the short ribs and cover tightly. Place in the oven and braise until ribs are very tender, about 3 hours.

3. Remove short ribs with a slotted spoon into a baking dish, cover and keep warm, or cool and then refrigerate, covered, overnight for up to two days. Strain the cooking liquid and discard the solids.

CHAPTER 5 • ENTRÉES

If you are serving them right away skim fat from the top and pour into a sauce pan. If you are serving later, refrigerate the cooking liquid overnight. The fat will have solidified and can easily be removed from the top.

4. Return the sauce to the stove top and bring to a boil. Boil until reduced by half to about two quarts. Season to taste. Mix the cornstarch and water until smooth to make slurry. Stir into sauce.

Serves 6-8

Short ribs can be difficult to understand. You will usually find them bone-in but they are available in many ways. The short rib comes from 3 different primal cuts on a steer; chuck, plate, and brisket. The ribs from the chuck will be more tender, as they see a lot less exercise. The ribs cut from the plate are the most common, but will be tougher. I like to use the "boneless short ribs", cut from the brisket. I buy mine at Costco, but any will work. For the most part short ribs lend themselves well to slow and low cooking - because of the fat content you will enhance the cut by allowing the fat to penetrate the meat slowly.

Chapter 6
DESSERTS

Mud Pie Cheesecake   page **148**

Apple Spice Cake   page **150**

**Pumpkin Bread Pudding
with Brandied Hard Sauce
& Cinnamon Whipped Cream**
    page **152**

**Apricot, Peach & White Chocolate
Blondies**   page **155**

Granola S'more Bars   page **156**

**Mocha Truffle Cake
with Espresso Whipped Cream**
    page **158**

**Chocolate Basil Tart
with Parmesan Ice Cream**   page **160**

Nectarine & Blackberry Cobbler
    page **162**

**My Favorite Hot Fudge Sundae
with Honeycomb Crumble**   page **164**

**Plum Galette
with Gorgonzola Walnut Streusel**
    page **166**

CAHOOTS TOO

Mud Pie Cheesecake

I like to throw this cake in the freezer a couple of hours before serving and serve it frozen or just slightly thawed, with hot fudge sauce, whipped cream and toasted almonds.

CHOCOLATE CRUMB CRUST
4 tablespoons unsalted butter

1½ cups chocolate wafer cookie crumbs

1 tablespoon sugar

1 pound malted milk balls

FILLING
1½ pounds cream cheese, room temperature

1 cup sugar

3 eggs + 1 egg yolk

1½ cups sour cream

2 tablespoons instant espresso powder

1 teaspoon vanilla

GARNISH
2 cups whipped cream

1 cup Hot Fudge Sauce, page 164

1 cup toasted sliced almonds

Preheat oven to 350° F.

1. Melt butter and add to the chocolate cookie crumbs and sugar. Mix well and press into a 9" spring form pan. Add the malted milk balls to the bottom of the crust.

2. In A food processor, add the cream cheese and the sugar. Process until smooth. Add the eggs and egg yolk and process briefly, scraping down the sides, until smooth. Add the sour cream, espresso powder and vanilla and pulse to combine. Let sit for a minute between pulses to dissolve the espresso powder.

3. Pour the batter into the spring form pan. Bake for 50-60 minutes, until the outside edge is puffed and the center is set. Turn off the oven, crack the door of the oven half open and let the cheesecake slowly cool down, for about 15 minutes. Remove from oven, cool to room temperature and refrigerate.

4. Garnish with whipped cream, Hot Fudge Sauce and toasted almonds.

Serves 16-18

Chapter 6 • Desserts

CAHOOTS TOO

Apple Spice Cake

I'm not a big dessert person, but, I have my favs. This would be one of them.

CAKE

2 cups all-purpose flour

2 teaspoons baking soda

1½ teaspoons salt

1 teaspoon cinnamon

1 teaspoon ground allspice

1 teaspoon ground nutmeg, fresh is awesome

¼ teaspoon ground cloves

1 cup unsalted butter, softened

1 cup light brown sugar, packed

½ cup sugar

6 eggs

1 teaspoon vanilla extract

4 cups Granny Smith apples, peeled, cored and grated

1 cup pecans, toasted and chopped

CREAM CHEESE FROSTING

1 pound cream cheese

¼ pound (1 stick) unsalted butter

3 cups powdered sugar, sifted

1 teaspoon vanilla extract

FOR THE CREAM CHEESE FROSTING

1. Beat together the cream cheese and butter until smooth, add the powdered sugar and vanilla and mix until blended.

Preheat oven to 325° F.

FOR THE APPLE SPICE CAKE

1. Prepare 3 9" cake pans with non-stick spray or butter and lightly flour them.

2. Sift together flour, baking soda, salt, and spices.

3. In a mixing bowl combine butter and sugars and beat unti creamy. Slowly add in the eggs, one at a time until blended. Add vanilla extract. Scrape down the sides of the mixing bowl, slowly add the flour mixture and continue mixing until smooth. Stir in the apples.

4. Divide the batter evenly between the 3 pans. Bake for 30 to 35 minutes until the cake springs back when lightly touched. Cool cakes, when cool enough to handle, remove cakes from pans.

5. Frost one layer of the cake and sprinkle with ¼ cup pecans. Repeat with next layer then frost the entire cake. Top with the remaining chopped pecans.

Serves 10-12

Chapter 6 • Desserts

CAHOOTS TOO

Pumpkin Bread Pudding
with Brandied Hard Sauce & Cinnamon Whipped Cream

This recipe was created for a Fall wedding here in Paso Robles, and the bride wanted a specific Pumpkin Bread Pudding that she and her fiancé had had at a memorable occasion. The pressure was on to re-create it, and we out did the predecessor.

8 cups Pumpkin Bread (recipe follows) cubed into ½" pieces

4 cups cinnamon bread cubed into ½" pieces

5 eggs

3 egg yolks

2 cup heavy cream

1 cup whole milk

1½ teaspoons vanilla extract

½ cup sugar

¼ cup pure maple syrup

1 cup pumpkin puree

2 tablespoons bourbon

1 teaspoon pumpkin pie spice

BRANDIED HARD SAUCE (recipe follows)

CINNAMON WHIPPED CREAM (recipe follows)

1. Preheat oven to 325° F. Butter a 13" x 9" inch baking dish. Spread cubed breads on a baking sheet and bake for about 20 minutes, turning once, until lightly toasted.

2. Lightly whip eggs and egg yolks. Add cream, milk, vanilla, sugar, maple syrup, pumpkin puree, bourbon and pumpkin pie spice, mix well.

3. Add the cubed breads to buttered baking dish. Pour the batter over the bread mixture. Press down on the bread mixture for even coverage over the cubed breads. Let rest for about 20 minutes.

4. Bake until slightly puffed and the center should be just set. Let rest for 20 minutes.

5. Drizzle the bread pudding with the brandied hard sauce and serve with cinnamon whipped cream.

Serves 14-16

Chapter 6 • Desserts

153

Pumpkin Bread

- 1¾ cups all-purpose flour
- ½ teaspoon salt
- 1 teaspoon baking soda
- ½ teaspoon baking powder
- 2 teaspoons pumpkin pie spice
- ¼ teaspoon ground cloves
- 4 tablespoons unsalted butter, softened
- 1½ cups sugar
- ¼ cup vegetable oil
- 1 cup canned pumpkin puree
- 2 eggs
- ⅔ cup buttermilk

1. Preheat oven to 350° F. Butter a 13" x 9" baking dish.
2. Mix together the first six dry ingredients in a bowl.
3. Beat butter, sugar and oil in a bowl at high speed until light and fluffy, scraping down the sides and bottom of the bowl.
4. Add the pumpkin puree and blend until combined. Add eggs mix until combined. Mixing on low speed, slowly add the flour mixture, then add buttermilk and mix until combined.
5. Spread batter in prepared pan and bake for about 45 minutes or until a toothpick inserted in the middle comes out clean. Cool completely before cutting into cubes.

Brandied Hard Sauce

- ½ cup unsalted butter, softened
- 1½ cups confectioners' sugar, sifted
- 2 tablespoons brandy
- 1 teaspoon vanilla extract

1. Whip ingredients until combined.

Cinnamon Whipped Cream

- 2 cups whipping cream
- ½-1 cup confectioners' sugar (to taste)
- 1-2 teaspoons cinnamon (to taste)

1. Whip all ingredients until stiff.

CHAPTER 6 • DESSERTS

Apricot, Peach & White Chocolate Blondies

Feel free to use fresh apricots and peaches when in season.

2 cups all-purpose flour + 2 tablespoons for dusting pan

1 teaspoon baking powder

¼ teaspoon baking soda

1 teaspoon salt

½ cup (1 stick) unsalted butter

2 cups brown sugar

2 eggs

2 teaspoons vanilla extract

1 cup macadamia nuts, coarsely chopped

1 15-ounce can apricot halves, drained & coarsely chopped

8 ounces frozen sliced peaches, thawed and coarsely chopped

4 ounces white chocolate, chopped

Preheat oven to 325° F.

1. Butter a 13" x 9" x 2" baking dish and lightly dust with flour.

2. Sift together the flour, baking powder, baking soda, and salt in a mixing bowl.

3. In a separate bowl, beat the butter and brown sugar until fluffy. Beat in eggs one at a time. Add vanilla and blend. Add flour mixture and beat until blended. Stir in macadamia nuts, apricots and peaches.

4. Spoon batter into prepared pan and spread evenly. Bake for about 50 to 60 minutes until golden brown and a tooth pick inserted in the center comes out clean.

5. After they have cooled, melt the white chocolate over a double boiler. Cut the Blondies into squares and drizzle with melted white chocolate.

Makes 12 (3" x 3") or 24 (2" x 2") squares

Cahoots Too

Granola S'more Bars

1¼ pound butter

1 cup light brown sugar, packed

1¼ cups dark corn syrup

7 cups rolled oats

1¾ cups all-purpose flour

3½ cups graham cracker crumbs

2 teaspoons salt

4 cups good quality dark chocolate chips

3½ cups mini marshmallows

Preheat oven to 350° F.

1. Butter a 17" x 12" baking sheet.

2. In a medium sauce pan over medium heat add the butter, brown sugar and dark corn syrup, until the sugar is dissolved. Remove from heat and cool.

3. In a bowl add rolled oats, flour, graham crackers and salt. Mix to combine. Stir in the butter/sugar mixture.

4. Press half of the mixture onto the prepared baking sheet. Top with and even layer of chocolate chips, then an even layer of marshmallows. Top with remaining oat mixture, pressing it in as evenly as possible, there should be some chocolate and marshmallows peeking through. This will be sticky so keep a dish of warm water handy to dip your fingers.

5. Bake the bars for 20-25 minutes until golden brown and bubbly. Cool slightly before cutting, but I recommend cutting them while they are still slightly warm.

Makes 24 3" or 48 2" squares

Chapter 6 • Desserts

Cahoots Too

Mocha Truffle Cake
with Espresso Whipped Cream

CAKE
¾ cup espresso or very strong coffee

1 pound good quality dark chocolate, chopped

1 cup sugar

¾ pound unsalted butter, at room temperature

6 eggs, at room temperature

ESPRESSO WHIPPED CREAM
1 tablespoon vanilla extract

1½ cups heavy cream

2 tablespoons confectioners' sugar

½ teaspoon vanilla extract

1 tablespoon instant espresso

Preheat oven to 350° F.

FOR THE CAKE
1. Butter the bottom and sides of a 9" spring form pan. Lightly dust with flour, shake out any extra.

2. Heat coffee in a sauce pan until it starts to simmer. Turn off heat and add chopped chocolate. Stir until melted.

3. Using an electric mixer or stand mixer, whip together the sugar and butter, until fluffy, about 1 minute. Add the eggs, one at a time. Add the vanilla extract. Slowly add in the melted chocolate and mix to incorporate. Pour into prepared pan and smooth the top.

4. Bake for 50-60 minutes, until the edges of the cake have puffed and the center is set. Cool for 20 minutes. Refrigerate for 4 hours.

5. Remove the sides of the spring form pan. Slice and serve with espresso whipped cream.

FOR THE WHIPPED CREAM
1. In a large bowl, whip the cream, sugar, vanilla and instant espresso, until it the cream holds firm peaks.

Serves 8-10

Chapter 6 • Desserts

Cahoots Too

Chocolate Basil Tart
with Parmesan Ice Cream

I came up with this idea in stages. First a friend gave me a chocolate-dipped basil leaf and I was amazed how well the flavors complemented each other. Later, I was in Tahiti of all places, and had Parmesan ice cream. This is a natural if you want to pair a nice red wine with dessert.

CRUST
3 tablespoons unsalted butter, melted

1½ cups chocolate wafer cookie crumbs

FILLING
1½ cups heavy cream

½ ounce fresh basil, chopped

10 ounces bittersweet chocolate, chopped

1 egg + 1 egg yolk

FOR THE CRUST
1. Melt butter and add to the chocolate cookie crumbs, mix well. Press into a 9" spring form pan.

FOR THE FILLING
Preheat oven to 350° F.

1. In a medium saucepan over medium heat and the cream and basil. Bring to a boil, remove from heat and let sit for 10 minutes. Add the chocolate to a bowl. Strain the cream, discarding the basil and pour over the chocolate, stir until melted. Let cool another 10 minutes and whisk in eggs.

2. Pour the batter into the spring form pan and bake 25 minutes or until filling is set.

Serves 8-10

Parmesan Ice Cream

2 cups half and half

¼ cup sugar

4 egg yolks

½ cup good quality Parmesan cheese, grated

1. In medium sauce pan over medium heat bring half and half to a boil. Remove from heat.

2. In a mixing bowl beat together the sugar and egg yolks. Add the half and half mixture, ¼ cup at a time, to the sugar egg mixture, whisking well. Pour the mixture back into the sauce pan and heat over medium heat until the mixture starts to thicken, about 5 minutes.

3. Remove from heat, stir in Parmesan cheese and cool completely.

4. Add cooled custard to the ice cream machine and process according to the manufacturer's instructions. Place in freezer until ready to use.

Cahoots Too

Nectarine & Blackberry Cobbler

FILLING
1 pound nectarines, about 6

3 cups fresh blackberries

1 cup sugar

2 tablespoon instant tapioca

BISCUIT DOUGH
1 cup all-purpose flour

1½ teaspoons baking powder

2 tablespoons sugar

¼ teaspoon salt

4 tablespoons chilled butter, cut into tablespoon pieces

⅓ cup heavy cream

2 tablespoons each of melted butter and sugar

Ice cream or whipped cream, optional

Preheat oven to 400° F.

For the Filling
1. Halve the nectarines, skin on and remove pits. Cut into ½" wedges. In a bowl toss the nectarines, blackberries, sugar and tapioca together. Pour into the bottom of a lightly buttered baking dish (9" or 10" round Pyrex® pie plate or 8" square one).

For the biscuit dough
1. For the biscuit dough, add the flour, baking powder, sugar and salt to the work bowl of the food processor, pulse a few times to mix. Add in chilled butter, pulse several more time to cut in the butter, about 6-8 pulses. On the last pulse leave motor running and add cream to make the dough.

2. Roll out the dough on a lightly floured surface to a 9" round, ½" thick disk. Cut into biscuits and set biscuits, touching each other over fruit. Brush with melted butter and sprinkle with sugar and bake for 25-30 minutes or until biscuits are golden and fruit underneath is bubbling. Serve hot, warm or at room temperature with ice cream or whipped cream.

Serves 6-8

Chapter 6 • Desserts

CAHOOTS TOO

My Favorite Hot Fudge Sundae
with Honeycomb Crumble

In my opinion there are certain things that are just better made from scratch and this is one of them.

REAL VANILLA BEAN ICE CREAM
1½ cups whole milk

1½ cup heavy cream

1 vanilla bean, split length wise

6 egg yolks

½ cup sugar

HOT FUDGE SAUCE
¾ cup heavy cream

½ cup dark brown sugar

2 tablespoons light corn syrup

¼ cup cocoa powder

¼ teaspoon salt

10 ounces good quality bittersweet chocolate, chopped

¼ cup unsalted butter, sliced into 4 pieces

1 teaspoon vanilla extract

FOR THE ICE CREAM
1. Place the milk and cream in a small, heavy saucepan. Using the tip of the knife, scrape the seeds from the vanilla bean halves into the milk along with the scraped bean. Heat milk over medium heat until it comes to a simmer. Remove from heat.

2. In a mixing bowl, beat the egg yolks and sugar until pale yellow and well combined, about 2 minutes. Slowly add the hot milk, ¼ cup at a time, into the egg mixture whisking constantly. Return the egg mixture back to sauce pan and heat over medium. Cook the egg mixture, stirring constantly, until the mixture is slightly thickened, about 5 minutes.

3. Remove the custard from the heat. Remove the vanilla bean pieces and discard. Cool and refrigerate until thoroughly chilled, about 2 hours, stirring occasionally. Pour the custard into the bowl of an ice cream maker and process according to manufacturer's directions. Transfer to freezer.

FOR THE HOT FUDGE SAUCE
1. Add the cream, sugar, corn syrup, cocoa powder and salt to a medium sauce pan, over medium heat. Cook the mixture until the sugar is dissolved. Increase heat to medium high and bring the mixture to a boil. Cook about 1 to 2 minutes, stirring.

2. Remove the pan from the heat and carefully stir in the chocolate, butter and vanilla. Whisk until smooth. Cool and refrigerate the sauce in an airtight container, for up to 2 weeks. Reheat over low heat before serving.

CHAPTER 6 • DESSERTS

Honeycomb Crumble

¼ cup water

1½ cups sugar

¼ cup light corn syrup

1 tablespoon baking soda, sifted

1. Line a cookie sheet with parchment paper.

2. Add water, sugar and corn syrup to a 1 quart deep sauce pan over medium high heat, stir well. bring to a boil, stirring occasionally, until sugar melts. Continue cooking, without stirring, until the syrup reaches 300° F on a candy thermometer, about 8-10 minutes.

3. Remove from heat and add the baking soda, stir 3 or 4 times. The honeycomb will puff up, climb the sides of the pan and turn golden brown. Pour onto prepared pan before it overflows. Do not spread it, it will stay puffed. Let cool to room temperature. Once cool, break the honeycomb up into pieces and store in an airtight container.

For the Ice Cream Sundae
1. All of these recipes will make more than you'll need – well, maybe! At any rate, to assemble each sundae, put one scoop of ice cream in a bowl, drizzle the warmed hot fudge sauce on top, and then sprinkle with some honeycomb crumble. If you want to get really decadent, you could even put some of the crumble in the bowl first as a crunchy surprise, or even add some chopped pistachios on top of the sundae.

Serves 8-10

Cahoots Too

Plum Galette
with Gorgonzola Walnut Streusel

I used Emerald green plums, but any variety will do.

Pastry crust, page 174

FILLING
6 purple plums, halved and pitted

⅓ cup brown sugar

½ teaspoon fresh rosemary leaves, chopped

STREUSEL TOPPING
1 cup all-purpose flour

¼ cup brown sugar, packed

½ cup walnuts, chopped

1 teaspoon ground cinnamon

½ cup unsalted butter, very cold, cut into small pieces

¼ cup Gorgonzola crumbles, very cold

1 egg yolk

2 tablespoons water

Preheat the oven to 425°F.

FOR THE PASTRY
1. Roll the pastry crust ¼" thick and 14" round. Place on baking sheet lined with parchment paper, refrigerate the pastry for about 30 minutes.

2. Whisk together the egg yolk and water to make an egg wash. Brush the edge of the pastry with egg wash.

FOR THE FILLING
1. Toss the plums with the brown sugar and rosemary. Pile the plum mixture in the center of the pastry round. Fold the pastry around the plums, overlapping the pastry, and press firmly to seal. Brush the outside of the pastry with egg wash.

FOR THE STREUSEL TOPPING
1. Combine the flour, sugar, walnuts and cinnamon in the bowl of a food processor. Add the butter and pulse several times to cut the butter into the flour mixture. Add the Gorgonzola and pulse a few more times.

2. Sprinkle the streusel topping over the galette. Bake for 10 minutes. Reduce the oven temperature to 325°F, bake for 30 minutes until golden brown. Serve warm.

Serves 6-8

Chapter 6 • Desserts

Chapter 7
BASICS

Marinara Sauce	page **170**
Aji Panca Sauce	page **171**
Herbed Goat Cheese	page **172**
Tapanade/Olive Sauce	page **173**
Cahoots Chipotle Mayonnaise	page **173**
Pastry Crust	page **174**
Lemon Aioli	page **174**
Tartar Sauce	page **175**
Basil Pesto	page **175**
Pico de Gallo	page **176**
Green Olive Aioli	page **176**

Cahoots Too

Marinara Sauce

In addition to the Baked Rigatoni with Italian Sausage and Creamy Marinara Sauce on page 105, this versatile sauce lends itself to a number of other dishes. Of course, it's great for spaghetti, but you can also use it for a topping for pizzas and bruschetta, or even to add an additional layer of flavor for grilled cheese sandwiches.

- ¼ cup olive oil
- ¼ cup fresh garlic, minced
- 2 onions chopped
- 1 bell pepper, chopped
- 2 stalks celery, finely chopped
- 3 28-ounce cans tomato sauce
- 2 28-ounce cans diced tomatoes
- ½ cup good red wine
- 1 tablespoon salt
- ½ tablespoon black pepper
- 1 tablespoon Italian seasoning
- 1 teaspoon dried whole oregano
- ½ teaspoon dried thyme leaves
- 1 teaspoon dried basil or ½ ounce fresh basil leaves, chopped

1. Heat oil in a 4- to 6-quart stock pot over medium heat.

2. Add garlic and onions. Cook, stirring until soft, about 2-3 minutes. Add bell pepper, celery, and cook for an additional 2 minutes. Add tomato sauce, diced tomatoes, red wine, and seasonings.

3. Reduce heat and simmer, uncovered, for about 2 hours.

4. Cool and refrigerate up to 5 days or freeze in portions you will use later.

Aji Panca Sauce

1½ ounces fresh garlic, about 12 cloves, chopped

1 heaping tablespoon of Gulden's® Spicy Brown Mustard

1 7-ounce jar of Aji Amarillo Paste (Amazon.com)

½ cup Aji Panca Paste (Amazon.com)

3 tablespoons lime juice

Zest of 1 lemon

⅓ cup lemon juice

3 tablespoons seasoned rice wine vinegar

3 tablespoons blood orange olive oil

1¼ cups olive oil

1 tablespoon salt

½ teaspoon black pepper

1. Add the first 9 ingredients to a blender or food processor. With the motor running add the olive oil until blended. Add salt and pepper, blend a little longer.

Cahoots Too

Herbed Goat Cheese

- ¾ pound cream cheese, softened
- ¾ pound goat cheese, softened
- 3 cloves garlic, chopped
- 2 teaspoons dried basil
- 2 teaspoons dried oregano
- 1 teaspoon dried thyme
- 2 teaspoons salt
- 2 teaspoons black pepper

1. In a mixing bowl combine the cheeses. Add the herbs and spices and mix well.

Chapter 7 • Basics

Tapanade/Olive Sauce

½ cup Pimento-stuffed green olives

½ cup pitted Kalamata olives

2 tablespoons capers, drained

2 cloves garlic, minced

¼ cup extra virgin olive oil

½ teaspoon black pepper

1. Add all ingredients to a food processor and pulse until ingredients form a coarse relish consistency.

Cahoots Chipotle Mayonnaise

1 ounce fresh garlic, minced, about 8 cloves

1 bunch fresh cilantro leaves, stemmed

¼ cup Gulden's® Spicy Brown Mustard

¼ cup balsamic vinegar

1 7-ounce can chipotle en adobo

2 teaspoons ground cumin

5 cups mayonnaise

1. Blend all ingredients together in a food processor. Add mayonnaise and blend.

173

Cahoots Too

Pastry Crust

1½ cups all purpose flour

½ teaspoon salt

1 teaspoon sugar

1 stick, 4 ounces, unsalted butter cut into ½" cubes and frozen

⅓ cup very cold water

1. Add flour, salt and sugar to a food processor fitted with the steel blade. Pulse a couple of times to mix.

2. Add the frozen butter. Turn on processor and pulse, allowing it to cut the butter and flour together (about 30 seconds) until the mixture resembles coarse meal.

3. With the machine running, add cold water until the dough comes together and forms a ball.

Lemon Aioli

2 cloves garlic, chopped

2 eggs

1 egg yolk

Zest of 1 lemon

Juice of that lemon

2 tablespoons Dijon mustard

1 teaspoon salt

½ teaspoon fresh ground pepper

2½ cups olive oil/canola blend

1. Add the first eight ingredients (everything but the oil) to the work bowl of the food processor. With the motor running slowly add the oil in a slow steady stream. The finished product should be the consistency of mayonnaise.

Tartar Sauce

1 cup mayonnaise (I use Veganaise®) or Greek yogurt

¼ cup red onion, diced

2 tablespoons lemon juice

1 teaspoon pickle relish, sweet or dill (I like sweet)

1 teaspoon horseradish

1. Stir all the ingredients together and refrigerate until ready to use.

Basil Pesto

2 cups fresh basil leaves packed

4 cloves garlic, chopped

⅓ cup pine nuts

¾ cup Parmesan cheese, grated

¾ cup olive oil

Salt and pepper to taste

1. Add basil, garlic, pine nuts and Parmesan cheese to a blender or food processor.

2. With the motor running, add the oil in a steady stream until blended. Season with salt and pepper to taste.

Cahoots Too

Pico de Gallo

2 pounds vine ripe tomatoes chopped

½ red onion, chopped

1-3 fresh chile peppers, Serrano, jalapeño, habanero, seeded or not, whatever you prefer, chopped

⅓ cup cilantro, roughly chopped

3 tablespoons lime juice

2 cloves garlic, minced

Kosher salt to taste

1. Mix all the ingredients together and refrigerate until ready to use.

Green Olive Aioli

2 cloves garlic, chopped

2 eggs

1 egg yolk

Zest of 1 lemon

Juice of that lemon

1 tablespoons Dijon mustard

½ teaspoon salt

½ teaspoon fresh ground pepper

2½ cups olive oil/canola blend

1 cup good quality green olives, pitted and coarsely chopped

½ cup capers

1. Add the garlic, eggs, egg yolk, lemon zest and juice, Dijon mustard, salt and pepper to the work bowl of the food processor. With the motor running slowly add in the olive oil to emulsify into a mayonnaise. Add the green olives and capers and pulse to combine.

Chapter 7 • Basics

Index

A

Appetizers
Artichoke Leek Squares 16

Asian Chicken Bundles with Thai Dipping Sauce 22

Beef Empanadas with Aji Panca Sauce 12

Crispy Prosciutto Crostini with Caramelized Onion & Pecorino 18

Grilled Chicken Spiedini 24

Herb Salad Spring Rolls with Dipping Sauce 14

Mediterranean Quesadilla 20

Sesame Chicken Skewers with Roasted Garlic Lemon Aioli 10

Shiitake Mushroom Spring Rolls 17

Artichokes
Artichoke Leek Squares 16

Steamed Artichokes with Lemon Aioli 56

Asparagus
Asparagus, Goat Cheese Prosciutto Bundles 58

Asparagus Soup with Goat Cheese, Lemon Crème Fraîche 30

Farmers Market Shirataki Noodles 108

B

Basics
Aji Panca Sauce 171

Basil Pesto 175

Cahoots Chipotle Mayonnaise 173

Green Olive Aioli 176

Herbed Goat Cheese 172

Lemon Aioli 174

Marinara Sauce 170

Pastry Crust 174

Pico de Gallo 176

Tapenade/Olive Sauce 173

Tartar Sauce 175

Beans
Black Bean, Corn & Feta 67

Cauliflower, Black Bean, Feta & Kalamata 74

White Bean, Tomato & Basil Salad 46

Beef
Bistecca alla Cahoots 140

Carne Asada (Grilled Skirt Steak) 139

Empanadas with Aji Panca Sauce 12

Jerk Spiced Mixed Grill Kebobs 124

Short Ribs 144

Simple Stir Fry 138

Steak au Poivre, George Munger's 143

Bread
Brioche Buns 84

Crispy Prosciutto Crostini, with Caramelized Onion & Pecorino 18

Grilled Panzanella Salad 48

Index

Rosemary Focaccia, with Caramelized Onion — 88

Schiacchata — 90

Winter Squash Loaf — 86

Brussels Sprouts
Roasted Brussels Sprouts with Pancetta, Dried Cranberries & Mustard — 62

C

Cheese
Artichoke Leek Squares — 16

BLT&P Burrata, Lettuce, Tomato and Pancetta — 94

Black Bean, Corn & Feta — 67

Crispy Prosciutto Crostini with Caramelized Onion & Pecorino — 18

Grilled Gruyere Sandwiches, French Onion Soup with — 32

Herbed Goat Cheese — 172

Layered Two Potato & Fennel Gratin — 78

Mud Pie Cheesecake — 148

Mediterranean Quesadilla — 20

Parmesan Ice Cream — 161

Ravioli Carbonara — 110

Southwestern Chicken Lasagna — 132

Spicy Buffalo Chicken Mac & Cheese — 100

Zucchini Brown Rice Gratin — 76

Chestnuts
Brandied Roasted Chestnut Soup with Fennel Confit — 35

Chicken
Asian Chicken Bundles with Thai Dipping Sauce — 22

Cahoots Club Cobb — 98

Cahoots World Famous Thai Chicken Salad — 50

Chicken & Eggplant Parmesan — 126

Chicken Provençal with Green Olive Aioli & Mediterranean Fritters — 134

Grilled Chicken Spiedini — 24

Jerk Spiced Mixed Grill Kebobs — 124

Lemon Chicken — 119

Sesame Chicken Skewers with Roasted Garlic Lemon Aioli — 10

Simple Stir Fry — 138

Southwestern Chicken Lasagna — 132

Southwestern Chicken Melt — 92

Spicy Buffalo Chicken Mac & Cheese — 100

Cod
(see seafood)

Corn
Black Bean, Corn & Feta — 67

Cahoots Corn Chowder — 34

Cahoots Too

Chocolate
(see desserts)

Couscous
Toasted Pearl Couscous
& Lentils   70

D
Desserts
Apple Spice Cake   150

Apricot, Peach & White
Chocolate Blondies   155

Chocolate Basil Tart
with Parmesan Ice Cream   160

Granola S'more Bars   156

Mocha Truffle Cake with
Espresso Whipped Cream   158

Mud Pie Cheesecake   148

My Favorite Hot Fudge
Sundae   164

Nectarine & Blackberry
Cobbler   162

Plum Galette with Gorgonzola
Walnut Streusel   166

Pumpkin Bread Pudding
with Brandied Hard Sauce
& Cinnamon Whipped Cream
    152

Dressings
(See Sauces)

Duck
Simple Stir Fry   138

E
Eggplant
Chicken & Eggplant
Parmesan   126

Grilled Vegetable Wrap
with Herbed Goat Cheese &
Tapenade   96

Layered Vegetable Casserole
    73

Mediterranean Roasted
Vegetable Fritters   66

Entrées
Bacon Wrapped Pork Loin with
Pomodoro Chimichurri   136

Bistecca alla Cahoots   140

Carne Asada
(Grilled Skirt Steak)   139

Chicken & Eggplant Parmesan
    126

Chicken Provençal with Green
Olive Aioli & Mediterranean
Fritters   134

Fish Tacos   122

Ginger Wasabi Scampi over
Rice Noodles   114

Grilled Leg of Lamb with Olive
Sauce   142

Costillos Adobado
(Grilled Mexican Style Baby
Back Ribs) with Grilled
Pineapple Salsa   128

Halibut with Avocado &
Lemon Aioli   116

Jerk Spiced Mixed Grill Kebobs
    124

Lemon Chicken   119

Salmon Wellington
with Fresh Herb Pesto   120

Seared Sea Scallops with
Baked Lemon, Pistachio &
Vanilla Risotto   118

Short Ribs   144

Simple Stir Fry   138

Southwestern Chicken
Lasagna   132

Steak au Poivre,
George Munger's   143

Sweet and Sour Pork Loin with
Tomato & Cipollini Onions
    131

Index

F

Fennel
Brandied Roasted Chestnut Soup with Fennel Confit 35

Layered Two Potato & Fennel Gratin 78

Fruit
(see desserts)

Grilled Pineapple Salsa 128

H

Halibut (see seafood)

L

Lamb
Grilled Leg of Lamb with Olive Sauce 142

Lemon
Lemon Aioli 174

Lentils
Toasted Pearl Couscous & Lentils 70

M

Mushrooms
Grilled Vegetable Wrap with Herbed Goat Cheese & Tapenade 96

Shiitake Mushroom Spring Rolls 17

Wild Rice Salad with Snow Peas & Mushrooms 60

O

Oats
Granola S'more Bars 156

P

Pasta
Baked Rigatoni with Italian Sausage & Creamy Marinara Sauce 105

Farmers Market Shirataki Noodles 108

Ginger Wasabi Scampi over Rice Noodles 114

Good Old Macaroni Salad 42

Jim's Favorite Pasta, Angel Hair with Roma Tomatoes, Garlic & Basil 106

Lisa's Favorite Pasta, Bowtie with Truffles 102

Pasta Fresca 104

Ravioli Carbonara 110

Southwestern Chicken Lasagna 132

181

Cahoots Too

Spicy Buffalo Chicken Mac & Cheese 100

Pastry Crust 174

Pineapple Grilled Salsa 128

Pork
Bacon Wrapped Pork Loin with Pomodoro Chimichurri 136

Costillas Adobado (Grilled Mexican-Style Baby Back Ribs) with Grilled Pineapple Salsa 128

Jerk Spiced Mixed Grill Kebobs 124

Pulled Pork Slider with Fiesta Slaw 95

Simple Stir Fry 138

Sweet and Sour Pork Loin with Tomato & Cipollini Onions 131

Potatoes
Layered Two Potato & Fennel Gratin 78

Roasted Fingerling Potatoes with Mustard & Garlic 81

Yukon Gold Potatoes with Roasted Garlic & Bacon 54

Pumpkin
Pumpkin Bread Pudding with Brandied Hard Sauce & Cinnamon Whipped Cream 152

Pumpkin Bisque with White Cheddar Sage Cheese 31

Q
Quinoa
Herbed Quinoa Pilaf with Summer Vegetables 72

Peruvian Quinoa & Forbidden Black Rice 64

R
Rice
Baked Butternut Squash Risotto & Burrata with Fried Sage 68

Peruvian Quinoa & Forbidden Black Rice 64

Seared Sea Scallops with Baked Lemon, Pistachio & Vanilla Risotto 118

Thai Rice Salad 61

Wild Rice with Snow Peas & Mushrooms 60

Zucchini Brown Rice Gratin 76

Index

S

Salads
Black Bean, Corn & Feta	67
Cahoots Spinach Salad	40
Cahoots World Famous Thai Chicken Salad	50
Ensalada Verano (Summer Salad)	44
Fiesta Slaw	49
Good Old Macaroni Salad	42
Grilled Panzanella Salad	48
Heirloom Tomato Salad with Gorgonzola & Kalamata	43
Jim's Favorite Salad	47
Lisa's Favorite Salad	38
Thai Rice Salad	61
White Bean Tomato & Basil Salad	46
Wild Rice Salad with Snow Peas & Mushrooms	60

Salmon
(see seafood)

Sandwiches
BLT&P Burrata, Lettuce, Tomato & Pancetta	94
Cahoots Club Cobb	98
Grilled Vegetable Wrap with Herbed Goat Cheese & Tapenade	96
Pulled Pork Slider with Fiesta Slaw	95
Southwestern Chicken Melt	92

Sauces
Aji Panca	171
Aioli, Green Olive	176
Aioli, Lemon	174
Brandied Hard Sauce	152
Cahoots Chipotle Mayonnaise	173
Chipotle Vinaigrette	47
Hot Fudge	164
Jerk Marinade	124
Marinara	170
Olive	173
Pesto, Basil	175
Pesto, Fresh Herb	120
Pico de Gallo	176
Pineapple Salsa, Grilled	128
Pomodoro Chimichurri	136
Tapenade	173
Tartar	175
Thai Dressing	50
Tomatillo	132
Tomato, Jalapeno, Mint Vinaigrette Dressing	38

Sausage
Baked Rigatoni with Italian Sausage & Creamy Marinara Sauce	105

Cahoots Too

Jerk Spiced Mixed Grill Kebobs 124

Scallops
(see seafood)

Seafood
Cod 122

Fish Tacos 122

Ginger Wasabi Scampi over Rice Noodles 114

Halibut 116, 122

Halibut with Avocado & Lemon Aioli 116

Mahi Mahi 122

Salmon Wellington with Fresh Herb Pesto 120

Scallops, Seared with Baked Lemon, Pistachio & Vanilla Risotto 118

Shrimp 114, 138

Simple Stir Fry 138

Shrimp
(see seafood)

Side Dishes
Asparagus, Goat Cheese Prosciutto Bundles 58

Baked Butternut Squash Risotto & Burrata with Fried Sage 68

Broccoli with Tomatoes, Fennel Pollen & Almonds 80

Black Bean, Corn & Feta 67

Cauliflower, Black Bean, Feta & Kalamata 74

Herbed Quinoa Pilaf with Summer Vegetables 72

Layered Two Potato & Fennel Gratin 78

Layered Vegetable Casserole 73

Mediterranean Roasted Vegetable Fritters 66

Peruvian Quinoa & Forbidden Black Rice 64

Roasted Brussels Sprouts with Pancetta, Dried Cranberries & Mustard 62

Roasted Fingerling Potatoes with Mustard & Garlic 81

Roasted Yukon Gold Potatoes with Roasted Garlic & Bacon 54

Steamed Artichokes with Lemon Aioli 56

Thai Rice Salad 61

Toasted Pearl Couscous & Lentils 70

Wild Rice Salad with Snow Peas & Mushrooms 60

Zucchini Brown Rice Gratin 76

Soups
Asparagus Soup with Goat Cheese, Lemon Crème Fraîche 30

Brandied Roasted Chestnut Soup with Fennel Confit 35

Cahoots Corn Chowder 34

Index

French Onion Soup with Grilled Gruyere Cheese Sandwiches 32

Golden Gazpacho 26

Pumpkin Bisque with White Cheddar Sage Cheese 31

Winter Squash Soup with Cheesy Crouton 28

Spinach
Cahoots Spinach Salad 40

T

Tomatoes
(see also Salads)
BLT&P Burrata, Lettuce, Tomato & Pancetta 94

Broccoli with Tomatoes, Fennel Pollen & Almonds 80

Ensalada Verano (Summer Salad) 44

Golden Gazpacho 26

Grilled Panzanella Salad 48
Heirloom Tomato Salad with Gorgonzola & Kalamata 43

Jim's Favorite Pasta, Angel Hair with Roma Tomatoes, Garlic & Basil 106

Pasta Fresca 104

Sweet and Sour Pork Loin with Tomato & Cipollini Onions 131

Toasted Pearl Couscous & Lentils 70

White Bean, Tomato & Basil Salad 46

Truffles
Lisa's Favorite Pasta, Bowtie with Truffles 102

Turkey
Simple Stir Fry 138

V

Vegetables
(see also Salads, Side Dishes, Soups)

Farmers Market Shirataki Noodles 108

Peruvian Quinoa & Black Forbidden Rice 64

Thai Rice Salad 61

Toasted Pearl Couscous & Lentils 70

Winter Squash Loaf 86

185

Cahoots Too

Table of Equivalents

LIQUID MEASUREMENTS:
Dash = 2-4 drops
1/2 cup = 1/8 quart = 1/4 pint = 4 fluid ounces
1 cup = 1/4 quart = 1/2 pint = 8 fluid ounces
2 cups = 1/2 quart = 1 pint = 16 fluid ounces
4 cups = 1/4 gallon = 1 quart = 2 pints = 32 fluid ounces
8 cups = 1/2 gallon = 2 quarts = 4 pints = 64 fluid ounces
16 cups = 1 gallon = 4 quarts = 8 pints = 128 fluid ounces

DRY MEASUREMENTS
1/16 cup = 1 tablespoon = 3 teaspoons = 15 milliliters
1/8 cup = 2 tablespoons = 6 teaspoons = 30 milliliters
1/4 cup = 4 tablespoons = 12 teaspoons = 50 milliliters
1/3 cup = 5 1/3 tablespoons = 16 teaspoons = 75 milliliters
1/2 cup = 8 tablespoons = 24 teaspoons = 125 milliliters
2/3 cup = 10 2/3 tablespoons = 32 teaspoons = 150 milliliters
3/4 cup = 12 tablespoons = 36 teaspoons = 175 milliliters
1 cup = 16 tablespoons = 48 teaspoons = 250 milliliters

TO CONVERT COOKING TIMES FOR CONVECTION OVENS:
Either lower the oven temperature by 25 degrees (long cooking, covered dishes may require reducing by as much as 50 degrees), or check the food about 3/4 of the way through the original cooking time.

Use the test your recipe gives you for doneness (*i.e.* internal temperature), and do not rely solely on appearance.

Table of Equivalents

What is a "GSM"?

This is a term you'll often see on wine labels and tasting notes. It denotes a traditional blend of three red Rhone wines: Grenache, Syrah and Mourvèdre. The exact percentages will vary, and you may even see a wine called "SGM" if the Syrah is the dominant grape. This particular blend is a successful trio because typically the "G" gives the wine a bit of brightness, the "S" offers structure, and the "M" lends notes of earthiness.

Wine Temperatures

It's been drilled into us that white wine should be chilled and red wine should be served at room temperature. However, many people make the mistake of serving wine too cold, which closes the wine up, or too warm, which makes it go blah. A good way to think about this is to think of how you react to temperature. If it's really cold, you're likely to bundle up and hunker down. Conversely, if it's a hot summer day, all you want to do is sit around and be lazy.

The ideal temperature for serving red wines is about 55-60 degrees F, the bottle should be a bit cool to the touch. For whites, it's about 50 degrees F, so if you've just pulled a bottle out of your kitchen fridge, let it sit about 10-15 minutes -- about when it starts getting some good legs of condensation running down the side.

WINE MEASUREMENTS:

- 375 milliliters = 1/2 standard bottle
- 750 milliliters = 1 standard bottle
- 946 milliliters = 1 U.S. quart
- 1.5 liters = Magnum = 2 standard bottles
- 3 liters = Double Magnum = 4 standard bottles
- 1 U.S. gallon = 5 standard bottles
- 4.5 liters = Jeroboam = 6 standard bottles
- 6 liters = Imperial or Methuselah = 8 standard bottles
- 9 liters = Salmanzar = 12 standard bottles
- 12 liters = Balthazar = 16 standard bottles
- 15 liters = Nebuchadnezzar = 20 standard bottles

Red Wine with Fish?

Red wine with meat and white wine with fish or fowl is probably one of the first "wine rules" we learn. Well, rules were meant to be broken! Salmon begs to be paired Pinot Noir, a rich duck dish would go wonderfully with a delicate Syrah, and grilled pork is a definite possibility for a Viognier or dry Riesling.

Don't Forget About the Beer!

With the rise of craft brewing (including several breweries here on the Central Coast), beer and food pairing is really coming into its own. Try a Pale Ale with a cheddar topped burger, a hoppy India pale Ale with spicy Asian or Indian food, or a Porter with smoked sausage. Also, many people think that beer pairs much better with cheese than wine does!

www.cahootscatering.com

Glossary

Aioli (ay-OH-lee): A flavored garlic mayonnaise from the Provence region of Southern France. It's a popular accompaniment for fish, meats and vegetables.

Aji Amarillo (ah-hee, a-ma-ree-oh): Aji amarillo is one of the most important ingredients in Peruvian cooking and is used in many classic Peruvian dishes. In Spanish "Aji" means chile pepper and "amarillo" is yellow.

Aji Panca (ah-hee, pahn-ka): Aji Panca is a type of chile pepper that is commonly grown in Peru and frequently used in Peruvian cuisine. It is dark red, mild with a smoky, fruity taste. It's often sold dried, or prepared into a paste. The dried peppers and jarred paste are found in Latin food stores.

Brioche (BREE-ohsh): This French creation is a light yeast bread rich with butter and eggs. The classic shape, called brioche á tête, has a fluted base and a jaunty topknot. It also comes in the form of buns or large round loaf.

Burrata (boor-RAH-tah): Burrata is a fresh Italian cheese, made from mozzarella and cream. The outer shell is solid mozzarella while the inside contains both mozzarella and cream, giving it an unusual, soft texture. It is usually served fresh, at room temperature. The name "burrata" means "buttered" in Italian. This deliciously creamy cheese is a specialty of Southern Italy, especially the regions of Apulia, Campania, and Basilicata. Traditionally made from buffalos' milk, today most burrata is made from cows' milk.

Carbonara (car-bo-na-ra): An Italian pasta dish from Rome, based on eggs, cheese (Pecorino Romano or Parmigiano-Reggiano), bacon or pancetta, and black pepper. Spaghetti is usually used as the pasta, however, fettuccine, rigatoni, or bucatini can also be used. The dish was created in the middle of the 20th century.

Chimichurri (chí mé-chu ré): An Argentinian sauce of parsley, oregano, chilies, lemon zest, vinegar, and olive oil, often served with grilled meat.

Cipollini Onions (chihp-oh-LEE-nee): Cipollini onions are smaller than conventional yellow, red or white cooking onions. In fact, the word cipollini translated from Italian means "little onion." Although its name is Italian, cipollini onions are used in a range of cuisines and dishes and are tasty eaten raw in salads or slowly cooked to release their natural sweetness.

Confit (cone-FEE): A technique for preserving meats such as duck, goose or pork that involves cooking the meat in its own fat, and then storing the meat in this fat in a covered container. The word confit can be used to refer to the technique. Today, it's possible to find restaurants that serve confit made from vegetables or fruits. These aren't true confits in the sense of a meat which is preserved in its own fat, rather, they're more like relishes, jams or chutneys.

Glossary

Empanada (em-pah-NAH-dah): Latin American pastries, filled with seafood, meat, cheese, vegetables or fruit are wildly popular. Thought to have originated in Spain, where the Empanada Festival is part of Galician culture, the name comes from empanar, or to coat with bread. Variations of this form of portable meals are found in Cornish pasties, Italian calzone, or turnovers.

Fennel Pollen: A rare luxury - tiny dried heads of wild fennel flowers. The spice has a sweeter and far more intense flavor than fennel seeds, meaning that a little goes a long way. Fennel pollen's nickname – The Spice of Angels – is probably a more appropriate way of labelling this spice.

Fingerling Potato: A small stubby, finger-shaped type of potato which may be any heritage potato cultivars. Fingerlings are varieties that naturally grow small and narrow. They are fully mature when harvested and should not be confused with new potatoes.

Forbidden Black Rice: The name forbidden rice may be because only emperors in ancient China were allowed to eat it, due to its rarity and high nutritional value. This black rice is a type of heirloom rice, meaning that it is open-pollinated, was grown at earlier times in history, and not grown on a large scale in modern agriculture. Forbidden rice can be found at many health food stores and Asian markets. The black color of uncooked forbidden rice is due to its outer coating of black bran. This gives the rice a rich nutty flavor when it is cooked, and adds to its nutrition, as the bran provides important dietary fiber. Forbidden rice provides other nutrients, including the amino acids common to most rice varietals. It contains phytonutrients, or phytochemicals, which provide antioxidants and other health benefits. In addition, this rice provides many minerals important for human health, including iron. Also known as Chinese black rice, this food is especially popular with vegans and vegetarians, but is beginning to gain popularity with a larger demographic.

Gazpacho: Usually a tomato-based vegetable soup, traditionally served cold, originating in the southern Spanish region of Andalusia. Gazpacho is widely consumed in Spanish cuisine, as well as in neighboring Portugal. Gazpacho is mostly consumed during the summer months, due to its refreshing qualities, cold serving temperature and availability of ingredients.

Jerk Spice: A dry seasoning blend that originated on the Caribbean island of Jamaica, after which it's named, and which is used primarily in the preparation of grilled meat. The ingredients can vary, depending on the cook, but Jamaican jerk blend is generally a combination of chiles, thyme, spices (such as cinnamon, ginger, allspice and cloves), garlic and onions. Jerk seasoning can be either rubbed directly onto meat, or blended with a liquid to create a marinade. In the Caribbean, the most common meats seasoned in this fashion are pork and chicken.

Pancetta: Pancetta is an Italian bacon that is cured with salt, pepper, and other spices, but is not smoked. Unlike English and American bacon, which are taken from the sides and belly of the pig, may be smoked, and are usually cut into slices, pancetta comes only from the belly, and is generally sold rolled up.

Pearl Couscous: Also known as Israeli couscous, is similar to regular couscous in that it's a small, whole grain-like food made from semolina or wheat flour. Because of its size, Israeli couscous has a slightly chewy texture, similar to barley, and, because it's toasted, it has a slightly nutty flavor. Like regular couscous and other whole grains, however, Israeli couscous is rather bland on its own, and needs to be prepared with seasonings, spices, sauces or fresh herbs.

Pecorino (peck-or-eeno): A hard, salty cheese made in Sardinia. Two types of pecorino are exported from Italy: Pecorino Romano made from sheep's milk, and Pecorino Toscano, made from ewe's milk. Pecorino is aged at least eight months or longer, which gives the cheese a slightly sharper taste than Parmigiano. It is often grated or cut into small shards and served on pasta dishes, but it also pairs extremely well with fruit.

Pico de Gallo: Translates from Spanish as the phrase "rooster's beak." It is a traditional Mexican fresh salsa. The principal ingredients of pico de gallo are fresh tomatoes, onions and peppers, usually fairly hot ones like jalapeños. Additional ingredients can include lime juice, cilantro, bell peppers, avocado, and garlic.

Pilaf (PEE-lahf): This rice based dish originated in the Near East and always begins by first browning the rice in butter or oil before cooking it in stock. Pilafs can be variously seasoned and usually contain other ingredients such as chopped vegetables, meats, seafood and poultry. In India they're highly spiced with curry. Pilaf can be served as a side dish or main entrée.

Pomodoraccio (A long, impossibly hard to pronounce, Italian word.): These are semi-sun-dried tomatoes marinated in a mixture of sunflower oil, wine vinegar, herbs, spices and seasoning, and they are oh so soft and supple. Handpicked and cut, each tomato is soft, juicy and packed with flavor. These super-convenient tomatoes can be used in so many different ways in the kitchen. They can do double duty as a topping for bruschetta and as an ingredient for a whole host of recipes instead of sun-dried or even canned tomatoes.

Prosciutto (proh-SHOO-toh): Italian for ham, prosciutto is a term broadly used to describe a ham that has been seasoned, salt-cured (but not smoked) and air-dried. The meat is pressed, which produces a firm, dense texture.

Quinoa (KEEN-wah): Quinoa was a staple of the ancient Incas, who called it "the Mother grain". Quinoa is not actually a grain but an ancient seed that is in the same family as spinach. Quinoa may be the ultimate survival food as it has everything your body needs- fiber, vitamins, minerals, healthy fat, carbohydrates, and is considered a complete protein because it contains all eight essential amino acids. Quinoa cooks like rice (taking half the time of regular rice) and expands to four times its original volume. Quinoa can be used as part of a salad, soup, side dish, entrée and even in puddings.

Glossary

Rice Noodles: There are several varieties of noodles made from rice, rice flour or rice powder, which are typically used in many Cambodian, Chinese, Japanese, Malaysian, Thai and Vietnamese dishes. Rice noodles are used in many dishes (stir-frys, soups and salad) and as an accompaniment to meat dishes. Rice noodles can be found in Asian markets, natural food stores and most supermarkets. Dry noodles are typically sold in coiled nests packaged in cellophane, fresh noodles are in plastic-wrapped trays in the refrigerated section.

Rice Paper: An edible, translucent paper made of dough formed of water combined with the pith of an Asian shrub or tree, appropriately named the rice paper plant. Rice flour is sometimes used. The paper comes in various sizes-small to large, round or square. Once hydrated, rice paper can be used to wrap foods to be eaten as is or deep-fried.

Schiacciata (ski-ah-CHA-tah): An Italian flatbread from the Tuscan region and usually on the sweet/savory side. Schiacciata is typically made during the late Summer grape harvest.

Shirataki Noodles (shee-rah-TAH-kee): Shirataki noodles are thin, low carb, gluten free, translucent traditional Japanese noodles. They are sometimes called konnyaku noodles. They are mostly composed of a dietary fiber called glucomannan and contain very few calories and carbohydrates. Shirataki noodles are made from Konjac flour, which comes from the roots of the yam-like Konjac plant grown in Japan and China. You can find them packed in water in the refrigerated section, in natural food stores and some supermarkets.

Tapenade (TA-puh-nahd): Tapenade hails from France's Provence region. This dish consists of puréed or finely chopped olives, capers, anchovies and olive oil Its name comes from the Provençal word for capers, tapenas. It is a popular food in the south of France, where it is generally eaten as an hors d'oeuvre, spread on bread.

Truffle/Truffle Peelings: A truffle is the fruiting body of a subterranean Ascomycete fungus, predominantly one of the many species of the genus Tuber. Some of the truffle species are highly prized as a food. French gourmand Jean Anthelme Brillat-Savarin called truffles "the diamond of the kitchen". Edible truffles are held in high esteem in Middle Eastern, French, Spanish, Italian, Greek and Georgian cooking, as well as in international haute cuisine. Truffles are ectomycorrhizal fungi and are therefore usually found in close association with the roots of trees. Black Truffle Peelings – perfect for the budget minded cook – are an absolute must for anyone's pantry. They can easily add a bit of flair and sophistication to the right dish. Perfect for flavoring pasta sauces, polentas and risottos.

Notes